Praise for Books by Dale Carlson

"The psychological-scientific wisdom of Carlson makes this a sophisticated survey that's very easy to read…'It's not what others tell you, but what conclusions you come to based on abundant information and common sense,' she says. Carlson grapples intelligently and passionately with such difficult topics as drugs, science, ethics, ecology, and the physical universe."

— *The Book Reader*

Peers Review *Who Said What? Philosophy Quotes for Teens*

"In a time of such world conflict…it is natural to seek to understand the nature of other people…to find common ground in the hope of ending misunderstanding…Just as in her book *In and Out of Your Mind: Teen Science* Dale Carlson's new book *Who Said What?*, has located the common threads of Eastern and Western thought, old thought and new, and compiled them into one work…This book encourages those who live only in conformity not to give in."

— Eric Fox, 17, Teen Editorial Director

"Words have a powerful effect on people. Perhaps no group is more aware of this than teens, people who are consistently bombarded with the words of their families, friends, and the media. *Who Said What?* provides teens with the words of the great minds of history in a way that allows them to be related to the pressures of growing up."

— Adam Crowley, 17

"A wonderful resource, whether you want a new perspective on an old issue or a quote to support your opinions."

— Alyssa Fox, 17

"The quotes in the book are drawn from sources that can be understood and related to by teenagers."

— Jessica Baycroft, 17

In and Out of Your Mind: Teen Science, Human Bites

"Contemplating the connectivity of the universe, atoms, physics, and other scientific wonders is heady stuff. Add human beings and their biology, philosophies...ethics and the result is this oddly-titled yet thought-provoking guide. Carlson delves into the mysteries of...outer and inner space in an approachable way...drawings are informational, humorous...quirky cover of a teen dressed as a cave man, playing guitar and crooning to the cosmos."
— *School Library Journal*

"Carlson explains science...in terms that teens can understand...and challenges her readers with questions to make them think about the environment, humankind's place in the world, and how ordinary people can...change things..."
— *Voice of Youth Advocates*

"Dale Carlson has written over 50 books, and she is deeply committed to opening up young minds. This is quite a book—just the names of the scientists and writers here will help with a reading program...a sophisticated survey that's very easy to read."
— *The Book Reader*

Stop the Pain: Teen Meditations
New York Public Library Best Books List 2000
Independent Publishers Award

"Five hundred years ago Dale Carlson would have been the village elder who, in the quietness and wisdom of her life, would have helped you see beyond the veil of the known."
— R. E. Mark Lee, Director,
Krishnamurti Publications
of America

"Much good advice is contained in these pages."
— *School Library Journal*

Where's Your Head? Psychology for Teenagers
Christopher Book Award
New York Public Library Best Books List 2000

"A practical focus on psychological survival skills…covers theories of human behavior, emotional development, mental illnesses and treatment."
— *Publishers Weekly*

Girls Are Equal Too: The Teenage Girl's How-to-Survive Book
American Library Association Notable Book

"Well-documented and written with intelligence, spunk and wit."
— *The New York Times Book Review*

"Spirited, chatty, and polemical, *Girls Are Equal Too* gives a crash course in gender discrimination."
— *Publishers Weekly*

"Clearly documented approach to cultural sexism."
— *School Library Journal*

Who Said What?

Philosophy Quotes for Teens

WHO SAID WHAT?
PHILOSOPHY QUOTES FOR TEENS

Dale Carlson
Pictures by Carol Nicklaus

BICK PUBLISHING HOUSE   2003   MADISON, CT

Director Editorial Ann Maurer
Associate Editor Danny Carlson
Book Design by Jennifer A. Payne, Words by Jen
Cover Design by Greg Sammons

www.bickpubhouse.com

Library of Congress Cataloging-in-Publication Data

Carlson, Dale Bick.
    Who said what? : philosophy quotes for teens / Dale Carlson; pictures by Carol Nicklaus.
        p. cm.
Summary: A collection of quotations from philosophers like Socrates and Krishnamurti, religious leaders like Jesus, Buddha, and Mother Teresa, and scientists like Einstein and Hawking intended to help one develop a personal philosophy.
Includes bibliographical references and index.
    ISBN: 1-884158-28-5
1. Conduct of life—Quotations, maxims, etc. [1. Conduct of life—Quotations, maxims, etc. 2. Quotations.] I. Nicklaus, Carol, ill. II. Title.
    PN6084. C556 W5 2003
    082—dc21
    2002023068

Available through:
Baker & Taylor Books
BookWorld Services, Inc. Tel: 800-444-2524: Fax: 800-777-2525
Quality Books Tel: 800-323-4241: Fax: 815-732-4499
Ingram Book Company
or: Bick Publishing House
    307 Neck Road, Madison, CT 06443
    Tel: 203-245-0073: Fax: 203-245-5990

Printed by McNaughton & Gunn, USA

Dedication

For my darling son, my firstborn, my first editor

Daniel Bick Carlson

Acknowledgments

To Edgar M. Bick, M. D., father, mentor, doctor, and philosopher, who taught me a passion for truth, and a fear of the false.

To Danny Carlson, M. B. A., son, friend, editor, and third generation philosopher.

To Ann Maurer, who has nurtured and provided editorial direction for Bick Publishing House books from the beginning.

To Virginia L. Rath, Ph. D., molecular biologist, with as sharp an eye for the details of writing as for science.

To Eric Fox, 17, teen editorial director, to Alyssa Fox, 17, and their senior classmates Jessica Baycroft and Adam Crowley—four peer teen editors, for their sharp minds and crucial comments.

and

To R. E. Mark Lee, Director of Krishnamurti Publications, and editor of *The Book of Life: Daily Meditations with Krishnamurti*, whose tempered wisdom and impeccable taste infused the conception and editing of this book.

❝ The ordering of the national life depends on the regulation of one's home life. **❞**

Confucius, *Ethics and Politics*

 **Who Said What?** ————— ———— ——

Books by Dale Carlson

TEEN FICTION:
The Mountain of Truth
The Human Apes
Triple Boy
Baby Needs Shoes
Call Me Amanda
Charlie the Hero

TEEN NONFICTION:
In and Out of Your Mind, Teen Science: Human Bites
Stop the Pain: Teen Meditations
Where's Your Head?: Psychology for Teenagers
Girls Are Equal Too: The Teenage Girl's How-to-Survive Book

ADULT NONFICTION:
Stop the Pain: Adult Meditations
Confessions of a Brain-Impaired Writer

with HANNAH CARLSON
Living with Disabilities: 6-Volume Basic
  Manuals for Friends of the Disabled

with IRENE RUTH
Wildlife Care for Birds and Mammals: 7-Volume Basic Manuals
  Wildlife Rehabilitation Series
First Aid for Wildlife

Contents

❝ …the question of why it is that we and the universe exist. If we find the answer to that, it would be the ultimate triumph of human reason—for then we would know the mind of God. **❞**

Stephen Hawking, *A Brief History of Time*

Introduction ━━━━━━━━━━━━━━━━━━━━━

Introduction

T his book is for people who are aware of their thoughts and feelings, but who don't always have the words for them.

This book is for people who have words for their thoughts and feelings, and want more words for them.

This book is for people who love to be right, and want more backup to prove it.

This book is for people who just plain love the language of words.

We humans are the talking-thinking animal. Thought and language are our species' survival tools, as speed, flight, physical strength are for other species. The advantages of thought and speech are that we can collect information and pass it on, personally and culturally, from person to person, group to group, generation to generation.

The disadvantage of words and language is that, inside the brain, they become ideas and thoughts, hundreds and thousands of thoughts—repeating the same things over and over, arguing with each other, driving you crazy. Thoughts, whether they are expressed as words or feelings, can be confusing. They can make you laugh, give you pleasure, bring you fear, anger, anxiety. They can store knowledge. They can induce happiness. They can torment. About ninety percent of our thoughts are the same as they were the day before, so they bring the comfort of continuity, especially those thoughts that produce the sense of the self.

Thoughts are like friends for most of us: close, constant, intimate as breathing, invading brain and body like the blood. Why not, then, choose good ones instead of bad? If we torment ourselves, sooner or later we torment others; family, friends, neighbors, other nations. It is inner war, that inner conflict of all the judgmental, nagging, angry voices in our heads that eventually explodes into outer war, as we take our anger out on others. Our relationship with ourselves, as well as with others, is what produces society, inner conflict producing outer conflict. Society isn't 'them' out there. Society is each one of us, just put together. Self-knowledge, the examination of our thoughts/feelings, is the basis for right action, the kind of action that brings joy to us all, not suffering, and therefore freedom to society and the world.

Here, then, are the comments of enlightened people—philosophers like Socrates and Krishnamurti, the great religious/psychological geniuses like Jesus and Buddha, scientists like Einstein and Hawking—through the centuries, who seem to have understood us better than we understand ourselves.

Try on and try out what these great thinkers say to see what fits. Don't just crowd the room in your brain with more stuff you can't use. If you find that what you read works for you, digest it, experiment with it, discuss it at home, in school, in conversations everywhere, in what you write, think, and do.

Thought is memory, the past. *Thinking* is done in the present. Empty the storehouse the brain has collected for hundreds of thousands of years. Let it observe everything as if for the first time, with no psychological authority. To seek an understanding of the complexities of the world and of ourselves, and to find joy and meaning in life, we must understand the machinery of our thinking, how it gives us security and pleasure, but also how it tortures us, how it separates us and alienates us from each other, how it sabotages our relationships to ourselves, with each other, with society, and with the world.

Technological memory, thought, science, medicine, electronic information— these things are helpful and necessary to everyday living, from remembering who your mother is to a computer password. It is psychological thought that torments us: the psychological authority of the should's and shouldn't's; the fears and prejudices of the past, our own as well as all the biological, racial, family attitudes of everyone before us.

Ways to Use *Who Said What?*
Use *Who Said What?* to compare the ideas of others, and in thinking them over, find out what you yourself think about these matters. Use it to change what you yourself think, and how you act, so you feel less often haunted,

conflicted, worried, frightened; so you feel more often free from the conditioned psychological reflexes, the knee-jerk thought/feeling reactions we all absorbed with our baby milk. If we can learn to put aside all the tape-recorded announcements from our species, all the racial, gender, cultural, and personal pasts (including yesterday) in our brains, we can look at what is really going on with new eyes.

You can use the thumb index to look up something particularly on your mind. You can use the index of authors and subjects to look up a particular theme or writer. You can read the book straight through as a philosophy book. You can use the book as a reference book about philosophers and their particular ideas—as each philosopher is introduced for the first time, name, occupation, dates, country of origin are given, and at the back of the book, brief biographies and main ideas of selected philosophers. Further reading is also suggested. And writing: use the **Your Philosophy** pages.

But however you choose to read *Who Said What?* at the end of each section, meditate on the word/theme of the section and find out what it means to you. You can use this book to inspire a book of your own by starting a journal to write down your own thoughts and feelings in response to what you read. Add what you find in your own brain and your own life to the wisdom of the ages. Even if you write everything you think and feel for only twenty-four hours, you will know yourself much better. And since all human beings have pretty much the same basic thoughts and feelings (even if they think and feel them at different times), you'll be able to use yourself to understand everyone else's brain as well as your own.

Who Said What? has been designed so that the great philosophies appear side by side according to subject. This comparative approach has suggested a startling insight: there is much agreement. There seems to be something special about the truth. What is true has to be true for everyone, or it isn't truth. Truth is fact. The words used to describe it may differ, but truth seems to be the same for every mind that finds it—and all minds are capable of finding it.

Dale Carlson, May 2002

A Vision

A ravishing ocean

A vision to eternity

We see winds rolling from the shores

Our brains are bruised with numb surprise

They call upon us, the ancient ones,

Only the chosen can hear their cry.

The gods are ravished and plundered

The ancient ones see the chosen

And the chosen ones break through

It's called the game of life.

Only a few dare to play it

The chosen see the world pass by like a flower gets blown by the breeze.

They shake dreams from their hair

And choose their door to eternal freedom.

We dive into the radiant ocean of divinity

And speak to two women Freedom and Pain.

They rise from the dead

And I keep expecting one of them to be effervescing with love.

Siddharth Shah
Age 14

" Give ourselves to each other until it hurts... We have been created in order to love and be loved. **"**

Mother Teresa, *No Greater Love*

Action ─────────────────────────

Action

Affection and Attachment

Anger

Authority

Awareness: Attention: Awakening

Action

Most people aren't looking for the truth about life, they are looking for someone to interpret life for them and to tell them what to do. We have been trained from our long, dependent childhoods to let someone else lead the way, to tell us what to do, and to take the blame when things go wrong. Can right action be based on the fears and prejudices of the past? Can it be based on someone else's authority? Can it be self-centered, or must right action be based on what is good for everyone?

Programming Minds

You know, we are always told what to think and what not to think. Books, teachers, parents, the society around us, all tell us what to think, but they never help us to find out how to think. To know what to think is comparatively easy, because from early childhood our minds are conditioned by words, by phrases, by established attitudes and prejudices. I do not know if you have noticed how the minds of most older people are fixed; they are set like clay in a mold, and it is very difficult to break through this mold. This molding of the mind is conditioning.

J. Krishnamurti, (1895-1986),
International philosopher
Collected Works, Vol. 7

The Basis for Decisions

When we grow older and leave school after receiving a so-called education, we have to face many problems. What profession are we to choose, so that in it we can fulfill ourselves and be happy? In what vocation or job will we feel that we are not exploiting or being cruel to others? We have to face the problems of suffering, disaster, death. We have to understand starvation, over-population, sex, pain, pleasure…and also that very strange and complex thing called love.

J. Krishnamurti
Life Ahead, Ch. 19

Action

The Act of Giving

Give ourselves to each other until it hurts. It does not matter how much we give, but how much love we put into our giving...We have been created in order to love and be loved.

Mother Teresa (1910-1997),
Yugoslavia/India,
religious philosopher
No Greater Love

Action without Violence

I have a dream today! Someday little black boys and little black girls will join hands with little white boys and little white girls and walk together as sisters and brothers. I have a dream today.

But don't get panicky. If you have weapons, take them home. We must meet our white brothers' hate with love...black people must use peaceful ways to fight for freedom... [marches, sit-ins, freedom rides... boycotts, and get the laws changed]. A lie cannot live forever...and segregation is a lie.

Martin Luther King, Jr. (1929-1963),
African American political/
religious philosopher
Speeches

Violent Action

It is wrong to aid and abet a national crime.

Let a white man touch me, and he dies; I don't boast this,—I don't say it around loud, or before the children, —but I mean it. I've seen them whip my father and my old mother in them cotton rows till the blood ran.

W. E. B. du Bois (1868-1963),
African American
political philosopher
The Souls of Black Folk

Act? Or Just Suffer

Hamlet. To be, or not to be: that is the question:
Whether 'tis nobler in the mind to suffer
The slings and arrows of outrageous fortune,
Or to take arms against a sea of troubles,
And by opposing end them? To die: to sleep;
No more; and, by a sleep to say we end the heart-ache....

Shakespeare (1564-1616),
English playwright and poet
Hamlet, III, i

4

Action: What You Do Seems to Be What You Get

...to be always on the move, learning, discovering, unfolding, is your eternal destiny. Living is life's only purpose...To live without self-concern.

Nisargadatta Maharaj (1897-1981),
Indian philosopher
I Am That, Ch. 29

Krishna, Moses, Lao Tzu, Buddha, Jesus, Mohammed—these, humanity's greatest philosopher/psychologists, all left suggestions for right action, the way of living that brings joy, not suffering

- *Moses: Ten and Other Commandments: Bible—Exodus, Leviticus (1200 B.C.)*

- *Lao Tzu: The Way of Life (600 B.C)*

- *Krishna: The Bhagavad-Gita: The Song of God (500 B.C.)*

- *Confucius (K'ung Fu-Tzu, Philosopher King): The Analects, I Ching (Book of Change, Commentary) (500 B.C.)*

- *Buddha: The Eightfold Path Dhammapada—The Right Path (500 B.C.)*

- *Jesus (Joshua): Sermon on the Mount: Bible—New Testament (ca. 20 A. D)*

- *Mohammed: Qu'ran (Koran) (600 A.D.)*

5

Action

Moses' Code for Right Action Is the Ten Commandments: He Summed It Up

You shall not hate your brother in your heart, but you shall reason with your neighbor...you shall love your neighbor as yourself.

> Moses (12th century B.C.),
> Jewish religious philosopher
> *Bible, Old Testament, Leviticus 17*

Right Action Comes from Right Attitude

If you never assume importance, you never lose it.

> Lao Tzu (born 604 B.C.),
> Chinese metaphysical philosopher
> *The Way of Life, 2*

Right Action Is a Whole (Wholistic, Healthy) Way of Life

Thinking about sense-objects
Will attach you to sense-objects;
Grow attached, and you become addicted;
Thwart your addiction, it turns to anger;
Be angry, and you confuse your mind;
Confuse your mind, you forget the lesson of experience;
Forget experience, you lose discrimination;
Lose discrimination, and you miss life's only purpose. [Bliss]

> Krishna (2, 500 B.C.),
> Indian/Hindu religious philosopher
> *The Bhagavad-Gita, II: The Yoga of Knowledge*

The Happiness of the World Is Based on the Actions of Each One of Us

A disciple asked, "Is there one single word that can serve as a principle for conduct for life?" Confucius replied, "Perhaps the word reciprocity (shu) will do. Do not do unto others what you do not want others to do unto you. "

Only an enlightened person knows how to love people and how to hate people.

Confucius (551-479 B.C.),
Chinese philosopher
The Wisdom of Confucius,
The Analects

Four Great Psychological Truths to Guide Action (Approximately Rendered)

1. We suffer: life, in constant change, hurts because we can't hang on to anything.

2. The cause of suffering is not life, it is our selves—clinging, trying to hang on to what passes, changes.

3. Food, clothing, shelter solve our body's needs. But the solution to our psychological suffering is freedom from the needy self.

4. The Eightfold Path (also approximately rendered) will help you not suffer .

   • Right Views—Understanding from the Four Truths that the problem is not the universe or life or nature or God or Goddess, but us.

   • Right Purpose—Self-interest, self-concern, self-importance are not it!

- Right Words—If you trash others, it haunts and hurts you as well.

- Right Action—Don't hurt! Yourself or others.

- Right Livelihood—However you make your living, don't harm anyone.

- Right Effort, Right Mindfulness, Right Connection to yourself, others, the universe—Eat when you eat, sleep when you sleep, pay attention to the whole of life, not just one little corner of it.

Buddha (563-483 B.C.),
Indian religious philosopher
The Dhammapada (The Teachings)

The Beatitudes Also Teach Right Action (Approximate Renderings in Brackets)

Blessed are the poor in spirit [those without arrogance].

Blessed are the meek [those without self-importance].

Blessed are those who hunger and thirst for righteousness [right behavior].

Blessed are the merciful [those who are forgiving—meeting a Nazi armband with a Nazi armband doesn't work].

Blessed are the pure in heart [examine your motives].

Blessed are the peacemakers [this does not mean passivity, doing nothing and letting the world go to hell: see the non-murderous, successful actions of Martin Luther King, Jr., Mahatma Gandhi, Jesus throwing the money-lenders out of the Temple].

8

ACTION

Blessed are those who are persecuted for righteousness' sake [see previous item, and most others quoted in this book]...You are the salt of the earth...You are the light of the world.

> Jesus (Joshua) of Nazareth
> (8-4 B.C.- ?-29 B.C.),
> Jewish religious philosopher
> *The Sermon on the Mount, Bible, New*
> *Testament, Matthew 5*

Don't Hurt

The Way of Heaven is to benefit others and not to injure.

The Way of the sage is to act but not to compete.

> Lao Tzu, *The Way of Life*

Beyond Me and Mine

Righteousness does not consist in whether you face towards the East or the West. The righteous man is he who believes in God; ...who, though he loves it dearly, gives away his wealth to kinsfolk, to orphans, to the destitute, to the traveler in need and to beggars, ...who is true to his promises and steadfast in trial and adversity....

> Mohammed (570-532 A.D.),
> Arabian religious/
> political philosopher
> *Koran (Qu'ran), Chapter II, The Cow*

9

Affection and Attachment

Affection is a tender, warm feeling, never infected with self-interest as attachment is, not dependent on another as attachment is. Affection is freely given; attachment is full of control, the fear of loss, the need not to be rejected. This is true among friends, mates, parents and children, teachers and students.

We Learn Less from Punishment than Joy, More from Affection than Fear

In education, it is my experience that those lessons which we learn from teachers who are not just good, but who also show affection for the student, go deep into our minds. Lessons from other sorts of teachers may not. Although you may be compelled to study and may fear the teacher, the lessons may not sink in. Much depends on the affection from the teacher.

J. Krishnamurti,
Education and the Significance of Life

When Attachment Comes in One Window, Affection Flies Out the Other

Your love and compassion towards your friends is in many cases actually attachment. This feeling is not based on the realization that all beings have an equal right to be happy and to overcome suffering. Instead, it is based on the idea that something is 'mine, 'my friend' or something is good for 'me'. That is attachment. Thus, when the person's attitude towards you changes, your feeling of closeness immediately disappears. Whether that person even becomes your enemy, your concern should remain...

Actually, genuine compassion and attachment are contradictory.

Dalai Lama,
Dalai Lama's Book of Wisdom

Affection and Attachment

Affection Is How We Feel and Behave, not Just Words

Peace and war start within one's own home. If we really want peace for the world, let us start by loving one another within our families. Sometimes it is hard for us to smile at one another.

Mother Teresa,
No Greater Love

Twisted Relationships

It is from our twisted relations with family, friends, and society at large that many of us have suffered the most...Either we insist on dominating the people we know, or we depend upon them far too much.

Bill Wilson (1895-1971), American founder of Alcoholics Anonymous
Twelve Steps and Twelve Traditions, Step Four

Affection Is to Live with Caring, not Depending on Results

...involvement without clinging. Not grabbing at anything. You may be attached to your lover: you say 'my woman' or 'my man'. There's the clinging. It can be part of the flow of the moment to be with a man or woman, but if he or she disappears tomorrow, that's a new moment. No clinging. Your life just lives itself...
I do whatever it is I do. I see people, teach, and write my books. I eat, sleep, and travel, get tired and irritable, go to the bathroom, touch, and taste, and think. A continuous stream of events. A flow. I am involved with it all, yet I cling to none of it. It is what it is. No big deal.

Ram Dass (Richard Alpert, 1931-),
American psychologist
spiritual teacher
*Journey of Awakening:
A Meditator's Guidebook, Ch. 1*

AFFECTION AND
ATTACHMENT

Anger

Anger based on fear of being hurt or because we have been hurt causes more trouble than any other motive. As a species we have inherited the brains of a violent predator, and our reaction to danger or hurt, whether to the body or our feelings, or cruelty to another, is to fight. Since anger is a chemical reaction in the brain and glands, anger just happens. It's what we do about anger that counts. By not allowing ourselves to act in the instant of anger, say most philosophers, we make time to act intelligently.

Like Hate, Anger Can Be Self-Importance

Anger has that peculiar quality of isolation; like sorrow, it cuts one off, and for the time being, at least, all relationship comes to an end...The anger of disappointment, of jealousy, of the urge to wound, gives a violent release, whose pleasure is self-justification. We condemn others, and that very condemnation is a justification of ourselves. Without some kind of attitude, whether of self-righteousness or self-abasement, what are we? We use every means to bolster ourselves up; and anger, like hate is one of the easiest ways. Simple anger, a sudden flare-up which is quickly forgotten, is one thing; but the anger that is deliberately built up, that has been brewed and that seeks to hurt and destroy, is quite another matter.

J. Krishnamurti,
Commentaries on Living, I, Ch. 30

Anger Mostly Poisons the Angry

Our country can be invaded, our possessions can be destroyed, our friends can be killed, but these are secondary for our mental happiness. The ultimate source of my mental happiness is my peace of mind. Nothing can destroy this except my own anger.

His Holiness, the Dalai Lama (1935-), Tibet's Spiritual Leader, Exiled
The Dalai Lama's Book of Wisdom

What Makes Us Angry?

What makes us angry are dangerously optimistic notions about what the world and other people are like.

Seneca (4 B.C.-65 A.D.), Roman Stoic philosopher, *Epistles* from *The Consolations of Philosophy* by Alain de Botton

Understanding Dissolves Anger

Surely that thing which you fight you become...If I am angry and you meet me with anger what is the result? More anger. You have become that which I am. If I am evil and you fight me with evil means then you also become evil, however righteous you may feel. If I am brutal and you use brutal methods to overcome me, then you become brutal like me. Surely there is a different approach than to meet hate by hate?...We have to understand the cause of our enmity and cease to feed it by our thought, feeling, and action. This is an arduous task, for what we are the society, the state is.

J. Krishnamurti, *Collected Works, Vol. 3*

By Humility, the Philosophers Suggest, not Passivity, but Selfless Action

Another question is that if you always remain humble then others may take advantage of you and how should you react? It is quite simple: you should act with wisdom or common sense, without anger and hatred. If the situation is such that you need some sort of action on your part, you can, without anger, take a counter-measure. In fact, such actions which follow true wisdom rather than anger are in reality more effective. A counter-measure taken in the midst of anger may often go wrong. Without anger and without hatred, we can manage more effectively.

Dalai Lama,
The Dalai Lama's Book of Wisdom

Three Intelligent Action Responses to Anger

If you see a man beating a child with a stick, take the stick away from him.

Ray Fisher (1936-),
American philosopher
Unpublished Works

Should I devote myself to the struggle for justice when the most needy people would die right in front of me for lack of a glass of milk?

Mother Teresa,
No Greater Love

Forsake anger, give up pride. Sorrow cannot touch the man who is not in the bondage of anything, who owns nothing.

Buddha,
The Dhammapada
(The Teachings)

Authority

My tremendous respect for teenagers lies in their search for truth, the need for understanding in the midst of confusion. Pain makes many adults glaze over the questions of life, why are we living, why do we hurt, and bury themselves in busyness and old answers that haven't worked for ten thousand years. There can be no psychological authority in the search for life's meaning, for whether there is God, for how to live. Obviously, we obey rules about courtesy, traffic, safety; freedom from authority does not mean freedom to do whatever we like.

Don't Take Someone Else's Word for How to Live

The more we are aware that we are lost and confused, the more eager we are to be guided and told; so authority is built up in the name of the State, in the name of religion, in the name of a Master or party leader.

The worship of authority, whether in big or little things, is evil, the more so in religious matters. There is no intermediary between you and reality.

J. Krishnamurti,
Commentaries on Living,
Series I, Chap. 30

Take a Fresh Look: Don't Use Even the Authority of Your Own Past Experience

Most of us are satisfied with authority because it gives a continuity, a certainty, a sense of being protected...But can I rely on my experience, on my judgment, on my analysis? My experience is the result of my conditioning, just as yours is the result of your conditioning, is it not? I may have been brought up as a Muslim or a Buddhist or a Hindu, and my experience will depend on my cultural, economic, social, and religious background, just as yours will...

I see there can only be one state in which reality, newness, can come into being...That state when the mind is

completely empty of the past, when there is no analyzer, no experience, no judgment, no authority of any kind.

J. Krishnamurti,
Collected Works, Vol. VII

Teachers Point the Way: We Must Walk the Way Ourselves

I won't teach a man [or a woman] who is not anxious to learn, and will not explain to one who is not trying to make things clear to himself [herself]. And if I explain one-fourth and the man [or woman] doesn't go back and reflect and think out the implications in the remaining three-fourths for himself [herself], I won't bother to teach him [her] again.

Confucius,
The Analects

Authority Is Not Yours or Mine, Anyway

Everything is determined...by forces over which we have not control. It is determined for the insect as well as the star. Human beings, vegetables, or cosmic dust—we all dance to a mysterious tune, intoned in the distance by an invisible piper.

Albert Einstein (1879-1955),
German/American
theoretical physicist
The Saturday Evening Post,
October 26, 1929

Psychological Attention to What Is Needed and When Tells Us What to Do

For everything there is a season, and a time for every matter under heaven:

a time to be born, and a time to die;

a time to plant, and a time to pluck up what is planted;

a time to kill, and a time to heal;

a time to break down, and a time to build up;

a time to weep, and a time to laugh;

a time to mourn, and a time to dance...

a time to seek, and a time to lose...

a time to keep silence, and a time to speak;

a time to love, and a time to hate;

a time for war, and a time for peace.

Ecclesiastes (3rd century B.C.), Hebrew philosopher
Bible, Old Testament, Book of Ecclesiastes 3

Outside Authority Does Not Work Anyway

Those who would take over the earth
And shape it to their will
Never, I notice, succeed.

Lao Tzu,
The Way of Life, 29

Seeking Truth, Not Authority

Science is the search for truth—it is not a game in which one tries to beat his opponent, to do harm to others. We need to have the spirit of science in international affairs.

Linus Carl Pauling (1901-1994)
American chemist
No More War

17

Awareness: Attention: Awakening

Can you take a shower by yourself, or a walk, without the company of voices of friends, your parents, the opinions of your own various selves, school problems, facts memorized for exams—all driving you crazy? We waste so much time and energy living in thought, our brains are so busy chewing over old information, we miss what is happening now in our lives.

Thought Is Just Memory: Pay Attention to Outside, not Just Inside Your Head

Attention is not the same thing as concentration. Concentration is exclusion; attention, which is total awareness, excludes nothing.

It seems to me that most of us are not aware, not only of what we are talking about but of our environment, the colors around us, the people, the shape of the trees, the clouds, the movement of water.

J. Krishnamurti,
Freedom from the Known, Ch. 3

We Live in Plato's Cave, in Virtual Reality, if All We Do Is Think

Imagine, says Plato, a group of prisoners chained immovably in a cave in such a position that their backs are toward the light that pours in through the mouth of the cave. They cannot see the source of light, nor the goings on in the outside world. All they see are the reflections on the wall in front of them. What do they really know about the sunlight and the world outside?

What the prisoners...people like you and me, fondly think is the real world...is actually only a shadow world.

Plato (428-348 B.C.),
Greek philosopher
The Republic, Book VII from
Ideas and Men by Crane Brinton

Thought Is Authority— Attention Is Freedom

Awareness is not self-improvement. On the contrary, it is the ending of the self, of the 'I', with all its peculiar idiosyncrasies, memories, demands and pursuits...

Awareness is to understand the activities of the self, the 'I', in its relationship with people, with ideas and with things. That awareness is from moment to moment and therefore it cannot be practiced. When you practice a thing, it becomes a habit and awareness is not habit...

Awareness is freedom....

J. Krishnamurti,
The First and Last Freedom, Ch. 8

Awareness Is Not Thought or Feeling

Your awareness is different from both your thoughts and your senses. You can be free to put your awareness where you will, instead of it being grabbed, pushed, and pulled by each sense impression and thought.

Ram Dass,
Journey of Awakening, Ch. 1

Awakening Is Tricky

The game of awakening is very subtle...You want to get rid of all your pain and have a little pleasure out of life. But you really don't know what you're buying. They say, meditate and you can have a Cadillac, but they don't tell you that when you get the Cadillac it's liable to feel a little empty. By the time you get to the Cadillac, who it was that wanted it isn't around any more. See the predicament? Meditation [psychologically waking up] changes your desires in the course of fulfilling them.

Ram Dass,
Journey of Awakening, Ch. 1

You Can't Pour Anything Into a Full Cup or a Full Mind

If your mind is empty, it is always ready for anything; it is open to everything.

Shunryu Suzuki (1905-1971),
Zen master
Zen Mind, Beginner's Mind

"Physical concepts are free creations of the human mind, and are not, however it may seem, uniquely determined by the external world. **"**

Albert Einstein, *The Evolution of Physics*

Body ─────────────────

Behavior

See: Action, Consciousness Is Conditioning, Relationships, Work

Body

Brain

Body

The most important body part is the brain. It is not separate from the body. It is basically the body's recording and anticipation machine whose major function is to keep the body alive in the environment. There is no little person in there. Physical nerve circuitry receives information and routes it where necessary for survival. Memory circuits invent an 'I' for continuity and security. Sadly, the brain's invention of 'I' and 'you', 'me' as separate from everyone else, causes loneliness and violence.

[Human beings] experience themselves as being a black-box sitting on the surface of the planet Earth, equipped with sensors...Joe Blow [each one of us] is inside the box...he will usually experience himself as being just posterior to his own two most-used sensors, the eyes...his 'I' has a constant instrument display... called the body-image. 'Here' [the 3 dimensions] can be described by references to three axes...'Now' is a constantly moving display...A more technical way of putting this is that Joe experiences his 'I' as existing in a 4-space with three real dimensions [height, width, depth], and one imaginary dimension, time...

Philosophers, neurophysiologists, and psychologists have been... preoccupied with...an oddity of the I-experience, namely homuncularity, our conviction that there is a little man or woman inside us doing the observing, willing, thinking, and feeling...it appears to be...a learned mode of experiencing.

Alex Comfort, M. D., D. Sc.
(1920-2000), British biologist,
neuropsychiatrist
Reality and Empathy, Ch. 2

Because Our Body's Brain Cannot See Reality Directly, We Need Science, Mathematics, Insight

In 1781, Immanuel Kant pointed out that time and space are not phenomena or things, but ways of organizing data…Kant gave to what we now call 4-space…the title 'a priori'—an invincible way of seeing with which human beings are born.

This study—thinking of other ways in which thinking might take place—is called 'demonics', a demon being shorthand for an imaginary intelligence which does not process inputs in human terms.

Alex Comfort, M. D., D. Sc.
Reality and Empathy, Chapter 2

So: Body and Brain Are a Cast of One, Not Two

René Descartes's famous sentence… "I think, therefore I exist" …has led Westerners to equate their identity with their mind, instead of with their whole organism. As a consequence of the Cartesian division, most individuals are aware of themselves as isolated egos existing 'inside' their bodies. The mind has been separated from the body and given the futile task of controlling it, thus causing an apparent conflict.

Fritjof Capra, Ph.D. (1939-),
American theoretical physicist
The Tao of Physics, Modern Physics,
Ch. 1

Thought Is a Bodily Process, a Reaction to Memory, the Nerve Circuits

You see the brain has a tremendous affect on organizing the body. The pituitary gland controls the entire system of the body glands; also all the organs of the body are controlled by the brain. When the mind deteriorates, the body starts to deteriorate...They work together.

David Bohm, Ph.D. (1917-1992),
American theoretical physicist
The Ending of Time, Dialogues with J. Krishnamurti, Ch. 9

The Mind-Endowed Brain

The mind is a recently acquired subsystem of the hominid brain, designed to render the organisms' awareness conscious, knowing that it knows. The means of the upgrading is language, the neural technique that accesses and handles our brain experience.

Zoltan Torey (1929-),
Hungarian/Australian
neuroscientist philosopher
The Crucible of Consciousness, Perspective

Mind Is Body

I want to reiterate that the mind...is a biophysical entity, a subsystem of the brain that is exclusive to humans. It is anchored...to the brain-code and the neuron-code beyond it. It is not the spiritual construct of conventional thought or the seat of consciousness, but the functional component that boosts the ground state of awareness onto the reflective human plane...it's driving component language.

Zoltan Torey,
The Crucible of Consciousness, Perspective

Take Care: the Body/Brain Is Sacred Ground

Do you not know that you are God's temple and that God's Spirit dwells in you? If any one destroys God's temple, God will destroy him. For God's temple is holy, and that temple you are.

Paul to the Corinthians,
I Corinthians 3: 16

25

BRAIN

Brain

The human brain has two main capacities: thought (the response of stored-up memory) and attention, observation, meditation (looking directly without thought).

Thought Invents Self

Thought is really, if one goes into it, if one observes it, the response of memory; and without memory there is no thought, no thinking...

That 'me', that 'self' is created by thought, because if there is no thinking, there will be no 'me'. The 'me' is not created by some supernatural entity; the 'me' is created by everyday incident...

Surely, there is only thinking and not a center which thinks. But thought has created the center [the 'me'] for several reasons. One reason is that thought is insecure, thought is uncertain, thought can be changed...but man is always seeking a place of security.

J. Krishnamurti,
Collected Works, Vol. 13

Learning to Live without Security Is the Only Real Security

For me, this whole process of investigation into oneself is meditation. Meditation is not the repetition of words and formulas, mesmerizing oneself into all kinds of fanciful states...Meditation is actually this process of investigation into oneself. If you go into it deeply yourself, you are bound to come across all this, where it is possible to think without the center, to see without the center, ...to love without the center...you will find out for yourself a mind that is completely free, which has no fear...

J. Krishnamurti,
Collected Works, Vol. 13

The Primate Frontal Lobes (Seat of Judgment and Planning) Are Add-Ons, not Replacements for the Old Mammalian and Reptilian Parts of Our Brains—Our Primitive Instincts Survive

In the animal kingdom we hold to the view that the most highly developed species have proceeded from the lowest; and yet we find all the simple forms still in existence today...In the realm of the mind, on the other hand, what is primitive is so commonly preserved alongside of the transformed version which has arisen from it that it is unnecessary to give instances as evidence.

Sigmund Freud (1856-1939),
Austrian founder
of psychoanalysis
Civilization and Its Discontents, Ch. 1

Our Brain Cannot Process All the Particles the Universe Is Made of—So It Creates a Universe of Objects It Can Handle

Physical concepts are free creations of the human mind, and are not, however it may seem, uniquely determined by the external world.

Albert Einstein,
The Evolution of Physics

All Animals, not Only Humans, Are Aware, or They Would Be Dead: but Only Human Brains Are Aware that They Are Aware

Human awareness has escaped the trap of inaccessibility. The breakout is the result of language...I want to reiterate that the mind I am talking about is a biophysical entity, a subsystem of the brain that is exclusive to humans. It is anchored in its technicalities to the brain-code and the neuron-code beyond it. It is not the spiritual construct of conventional thought.

Zoltan Torey (1929-),
The Crucible of Consciousness,
Perspective

The Driving Component of the Mind-Boosted Brain Is Language

The mind is a recently acquired subsystem of the hominid brain, designed to render the organism's awareness conscious, knowing that it knows. The means of the upgrading is language, the neural technique that accesses and handles our brain experience...

Awareness has no special locus in the brain.

Zoltan Torey,
The Crucible of Consciousness, Ch. 1

Our Speech Habits Give Us the Feeling of 'Me' Doing It—A Phrase Closer to the Truth: "This Organism Sees You" Not "I See You"

What we colloquially refer to as our 'conscious mind' is really only the old primate brain revealed to itself and empowered by new techniques [speech, language] to take an active part in guiding itself and generating the awareness of being aware.

Zoltan Torey,
The Crucible of Consciousness, Ch. 6 B

The Human Brain May Be the Cosmos Unfolding Itself

As marvelous as the stars is the mind of the person who studies them.

Martin Luther King, Jr.
in *Voyage to the Great Attractor*, by Alan Dressler

The Gene's-Eye View

The mind is an organ of computation engineered by natural selection.

Steven Pinker (1954 -),
American cognitive neuroscientist
How the Mind Works, Ch. 1

The Nerds of the Earth

We are the brainy animal that fills the cognitive niche [but]…Evolution is about ends, not means; becoming smart is just one option.

Steven Pinker, American
neuroscientist, *How the Mind Works*

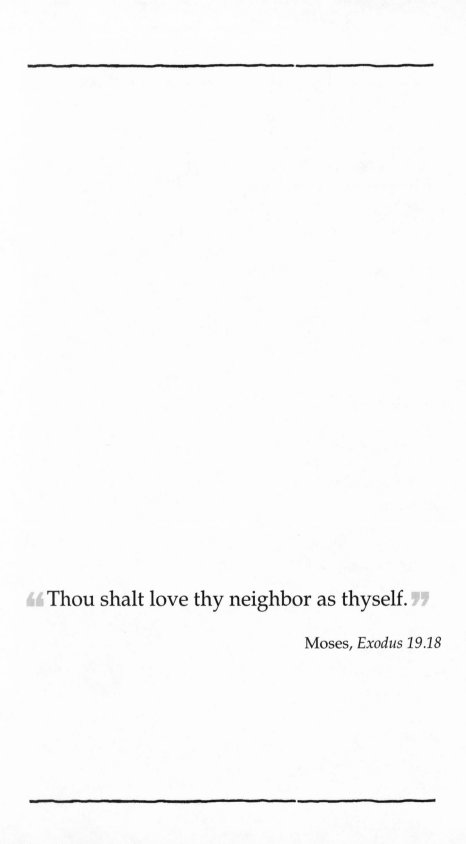

"Thou shalt love thy neighbor as thyself.**"**

Moses, *Exodus 19.18*

Confusion: Choice: Clarity

Consciousness Is Conditioning

Confusion: Choice: Clarity

The prison of consciousness is not hopelessly locked. Understanding the ways of the self, of consciousness, is the key to freedom—if freedom is what you want.

The Game of Awakening:

We have built up a set of ego habits for gaining satisfaction. For some it involves pleasure; for others, more neurotic, it involves pain...a living hell, but a familiar one.

This network of thoughts has been your home...safe and familiar... Because this structure has always been your home, you assume that it is what reality is—that your thoughts are Reality with a capital R.

If you start to use a method [paying attention to all this] that makes gaps in this web of thoughts of who you are and what reality is, and if it lets the sunlight in and you peek out for a moment, might you not be frightened as the comforting walls of ego [your particular species, cultural, religious consciousness] start to crumble? Might you not prefer the security of this familiar prison, grim though it sometimes may be, to the uncertainty of the unknown?

...For here is your choice: whether you truly wish to escape from the prison or are just fooling yourself.

Ram Dass,
Journey of Awakening, Ch 1

Choices Come from Confusion: Clarity Makes the Right Thing to Do Obvious

For God is not a God of confusion but of peace.

Paul of Tarsus (died c. 67 A.D.),
Jewish/Christian missionary
I Corinthians, 14: 33

Consciousness Is Conditioning

Consciousness is everything recorded in our brain, all the conditioning, all the agendas, behaviors, thoughts, reactions, information, opinions, fears that mold us. We carry in our consciousness whatever has adapted us for life on Earth, for life among other humans. We are programmed genetically and personally to respond to our environment. Differences between one human consciousness and another are purely superficial: understand yourself, you understand us all.

What Is Our Mind?

It seems to me that without understanding the way our minds work, one cannot understand and resolve the very complex problems of living...The mind is the only instrument we have, the instrument with which we think, we act, we have our being...

What is our mind, yours and mine?... The mind is divided into the conscious and the unconscious. If we do not like to use these two words, we might use the terms, superficial and hidden...the whole...is what we call consciousness...

We are made to believe in certain ideas from childhood, we are conditioned by dogmas, by beliefs, by theories. Each one of us is conditioned by various influences, and from that conditioning, from those limited and unconscious influences, our thoughts spring...Thought obviously springs from the background of memory, of tradition. Our minds are conditioned, held, tethered to dogma...

J. Krishnamurti,
Collected Works, Vol. 8,

We Call Our Program—the Self

Do we know what we mean by the self?...the accumulated memory of the unconscious, the racial, the group, the individual, the clan, and the whole of it all.

J. Krishnamurti,
First and Last Freedom, Ch. 9

We See the World Only Through the Veils of Our Limited Senses and Prejudices

Nature is objective, and nature is knowable, but we can only view her through a glass darkly—and many clouds upon our vision are of our own making: social and cultural biases, psychological preferences, and mental limitations (in universal modes of thought, not just individualized stupidity).

> Stephen Jay Gould (1941-2002),
> American evolutionary scientist
> *Full House, Ch. 1*

We See Earth, All Life, the Universe Skewed by Human Perspective

We crave progress as our best hope for retaining human arrogance in an evolutionary world [when] Homo sapiens…is a tiny twig, born just yesterday on an enormously arborescent tree of life that would never produce the same set of branches if regrown from seed.

> Stephen Jay Gould,
> *Full House, Ch. 1*

What 'You' Are Is the Program that Runs on Your Brain's Computer: 'You' May Be Just a Floppy or a CD

There is no self apart from thought which created it.

> J. Krishnamurti,
> *What Are You Doing with Your Life?*
> *Books on Living for Teens, 1*

Consciousness Is Conditioning

CONSCIOUSNESS IS CONDITIONING

Consciousness Is Not a Mini-Me—It's Just Information

The phenomena of human consciousness have been explained...in terms of the operations of a 'virtual machine', a sort of evolved (and evolving) computer program that shapes the activities of the brain. There is no Cartesian Theater [Descartes' ghost in the machine, a homunculus or mini-me sitting in the head, a 'self' taking in the world and thinking about it]; there are just Multiple Drafts composed by the processes of content fixation playing various semi-independent roles in the brain's larger economy of controlling a human body's journey through life...there can be conscious machines—us. Think of the brain as a computer of sorts...as information-processing systems.

Daniel C. Dennett (1942-),
American cognitive
scientist/philosopher
Consciousness Explained, Ch. 14

It is the Whole Organism that Thinks and Feels

The trouble with brains, it seems, is that when you look in them, you discover that there's nobody home. No part of the brain is the thinker that does the thinking or the feeler that does the feeling, and the whole brain appears to be no better a candidate for that very special role...The idea that a self or a person (or for that matter, a soul) is distinct from a brain or a body is deeply rooted in our ways of speaking, and hence in our ways of thinking.

Daniel Dennett,
Consciousness Explained, Ch 2

The Strong-if-Wrong Feeling of 'I' Is a Mental Magic Trick We Teach Children

The group is the behavioral setting in which the...brain of the human infant is able to develop its latent speech capability. Without the group and the exposure to language, the child could acquire neither speech nor internal communication (thought) and therefore reflective awareness [consciousness].

Zoltan Torey,
The Crucible of Consciousness, Ch. 2

We Do Not See Nature's Truth: We Translate It

A universal biophysical idiom, that is, a neural language...has evolved...for raw data into a user-friendly form. Indeed, if the brain (human or animal) would have to cope with the ocean of light waves, pressure waves and assorted raw data in which it is immersed, it would be overwhelmed and unable to make sense of it.

Zoltan Torey,
The Crucible of Consciousness,
Perspective

Plato Knew We Must Leave the Cave of Our Consciousness for True Insight: the Truth Is Out There, not Inside Our Heads

Behold! Human beings living in an underground den...Like ourselves... they see only their own shadows, or the shadows of one another, which the fire throws on the opposite wall of the cave.

Plato (c. 427-347 B.C.),
Greek philosopher
The Republic, Book V

"Even at the moment of death he is alive in that enlightenment: Brahman [God] and he are one.**"**

Lord Krishna, *The Bhagavad Gita: II*

Death

Death

Dependency and Desire

Depression

Death

[See also: Life]

Nothing in the universe dies, only changes: death is a word we have invented. As for physical death, the death of the body, what is it but a return of atoms to atoms? Everything is made of the same stuff in the universe, us and the trees and the stars. Nothing disappears.

Says Stephen Hawking, physicist, cosmologist, one of the great minds of the twentieth century, "There was a time, about ten or twenty thousand million years ago, called the big bang, when the universe was infinitesimally small and infinitely dense. Everything came from the exploding matter of that density, that ball of matter. "

DEATH

Science and Religion Question whether We and the Universe Really Die

...if we do discover a complete theory [unified theory of both relativity and quantum mechanics], it should in time be understandable...by everyone...of why it is that we and the universe exist. If we find the answer to that, it would be the ultimate triumph of human reason—for then we should know the mind of God.

Stephen Hawking (1942-),
English physicist/cosmologist
A Brief History of Time, from the Big Bang to Black Holes, Conclusion

Only the 'Me' Fears Death

In the dying of the 'me' every minute there is eternity, there is immortality.

J. Krishnamurti,
Collected Works, Vol. V

Death

God and the Universe Are Life, not Death

Does man think he will be left alone, to no purpose? Was he not a drop of ejaculated semen? He became a clot of blood; then God formed and molded him, and gave him male and female parts. Has He no power, then, to raise the dead to life?

Mohammed,
Koran, The Resurrection 75: 40

There Is No Death: God and You Are Already One

Even at the moment of death
He is alive in that enlightenment:
Brahman [God] and he are one.

Lord Krishna,
The Bhagavad-Gita: II,
The Yoga of Knowledge. p. 44

Live Rightly and There Is No Fear of Death

He leads me in paths of
righteousness
for his name's sake.
Even though I walk through the
valley of the shadow of death,
I fear no evil;
for thou art with me;
thy rod and thy staff,
they comfort me

David (died c. 973 B.C.),
King of Judah and Israel,
poet/philosopher
Bible, Old Testament, Psalm 23: 4

DEATH

Real Life Is Before and After: Human Life We Invent Like a Play

Our revels now are ended. These
  our actors,
As I foretold you, were all spirits
  and
Are melted into air, into thin air;
And, like the baseless fabric of this
  vision,
The cloud-capped towers, the
  gorgeous palaces,
The solemn temples, the great
  globe itself,
Yea, all which it inherit, shall
  dissolve…
We are such stuff
As dreams are made on, and our
  little life
Is rounded with a sleep.

William Shakespeare,
The Tempest, Act IV, Scene 1

We Are Made of Atoms—What Dies?

Nothing dies. The body is just imagined. There is no such thing.

Nisargadatta Maharaj,
I Am That, Ch. 7

Dependency and Desire

Desires are natural. It is dependency that causes problems. One problem is when we think we have to have everything we want. Another problem rises when we grow dependent on the people, or things, or substances we desire. We get fearful, and angry, at the possibility of loss.

Without Desire You Would Be Dead

Creation gave us instincts for a purpose. Without them we wouldn't be complete human beings. If men and women didn't exert themselves to be secure in their persons, made no effort to harvest food or construct shelter, there would be no survival. If they didn't reproduce, the earth wouldn't be populated...So these desires—for the sex relation, for material and emotional security, and for companionship—are perfectly necessary and right, and surely God-given. Yet these instincts, so necessary for our existence, often far exceed their proper functions. Powerfully, blindly, many times subtly, they drive us, dominate us, and insist upon ruling our lives. Our desires for sex, material and emotional security, and for an important place in society often tyrannize us. When thus out of joint, man's natural desires cause him great trouble...Nearly every serious emotional problem can be seen as a case of misdirected instinct.

> Bill Wilson (1895-1971),
> *Twelve Steps and Twelve Traditions, Step Four*

You Cannot Carry a Wall with You through Life: Learn Not to Lean

Our demand for emotional security, for our own way, had constantly thrown us into unworkable relations with other people...Either we had tried to play God and dominate those about us, or we had insisted on being overdependent upon them.

> Bill Wilson, *Twelve Steps and Twelve Traditions, Step 12*

What You Depend On, You Get Angry At

Grow attached, and you become addicted;

Thwart your addiction, it turns to anger;

Lord Krishna, *The Bhagavad-Gita, II The Yoga of Knowledge*

Chasing Romance with People in Passing Cars—Not a Good Choice

Those who are slaves of desires run into the stream of desires, even as a spider runs into the web that it made.

Buddha, *The Dhammapada, Ch. 24*

Desire, Wanting, Is Natural: It Means You Are Alive: Add the Thought 'Must Have More' and Pain Begins

You see a beautiful sunset, a lovely tree, a river that has a wide, curving movement, or a beautiful face, and to look at it gives great pleasure, delight. What is wrong with that? It seems to me the confusion and the misery begin when that face, that river, that cloud, that mountain becomes a memory, and this memory then demands...continuity.

What matters is to understand pleasure, not try to get rid of it—that is too stupid. Nobody can get rid of pleasure. But to understand the nature and structure of pleasure is essential; because if life is only pleasure...then with pleasure go the misery, the confusion, the illusions, the false values which we create, and therefore there is no clarity.

J. Krishnamurti, *Collected Works, Vol. XV*

DEPENDENCY AND DESIRE

Depression

Depression happens to children and teenagers as well as adults. Loneliness, sadness, grief, self-pity—these states of being are the painful discovery of our own empty feelings of being completely cut off from everyone and everything else. Because we have not been told that the mind is normally empty, that there is no self, the discovery of emptiness fills us with fear. Brain experts also tell us much mental illness, including depression, is due to biochemical imbalances. Psychotherapists tell us that death, divorce, the separation from someone important, loss, failure, shame—all these may be the cause of depression.

Feeling Bad Can Be a Terrific Teacher

At any moment, whatever we are experiencing, only one of two things is ever happening: either we are being with what is, or else we are resisting what is. Being with what is means letting ourselves have and feel our experience, just as it is right now...

Yet oddly enough, we rarely let ourselves simply have our experience. We are usually resisting it instead—trying to manipulate it...Yet when we contract ourselves against the painful aspects of our experience, we actually stop being...

When we habitually contract against an area of our experience, such as anger, it's as though we create a hole or dead spot in our being. Then when anger arises—in ourselves or in others—we go dead...

John Welwood (1941-),
American psychotherapist
*Ordinary Magic: Everyday Life
as Spiritual Path*

**Understanding Your Sad
Feelings Can End Them:
Escape into Drugs, Sex, Food
and You're Still Sad, Only Now
You're an Addict, Fat, and in
Trouble As Well**

Not everything which makes us feel
better is good for us. Not everything
which hurts may be bad.

Friedrich Nietzsche (1844-1900),
German philosopher
Ecce Homo, Ch. 14

The greatest fear about depression is that it will never end. To see that we can be alone, empty without fear, is to see the truth. Once you see it, you'll never panic again. Lonely feelings will simply turn into the pleasure of being alone. People will come into your life and go. Things will come into your life and go. The tides come in. The tides go out, and you're fine. They'll come in again. They always do.

47

❝ Men have gained control over the forces of nature to such an extent that with their help they could have no difficulty in exterminating one another to the last man. They know this, and hence comes a large part of their current unrest, their unhappiness, and their mood of anxiety. ❞

Sigmund Freud, *Civilization and Its Discontents*

Education

Education

Evil

Education

What is education? From the Latin it means to draw out, not stuff in. It means to help students discover themselves and their interests, not just condition them to validate their elders. A big part of education is to show us how inner images distort outer reality.

Our Children Are Not Ours to Own

It is only when we begin to understand the deep significance of human life that there can be true education; but to understand, the mind must intelligently free itself from the desire for reward which breeds fear and conformity. If we regard our children as personal property, if to us they are the continuance of our petty selves and the fulfillment of our ambitions, then we shall build an environment, a social structure in which there is no love, but only the pursuit of self-centered advantages.

J. Krishnamurti,
Education and the Significance of Life, Ch. 5

We Must Learn Technique, Technology, to Earn a Living: Not to Harm

Men have gained control over the forces of nature to such an extent that with their help they could have no difficulty in exterminating one another to the last man. They know this, and hence comes a large part of their current unrest, their unhappiness, and their mood of anxiety.

Sigmund Freud,
Civilization and Its Discontents, VIII

Education

Education Is to Learn the Ways of Our Human Self—to Examine Our Motives

This odd trait of mind and emotion, this perverse wish to hide a bad motive underneath a good one, permeates human affairs from top to bottom. This subtle and elusive kind of self-righteousness can underlie the smallest act or thought.

Bill Wilson, *Twelve Steps and Twelve Traditions, Step Ten*

Education: To Find Out What Interests You to Do, What You Are Good at

Let early education be a sort of amusement; you will then be better able to find out the natural bent.

Plato, *The Republic, Book I, 537*

What You Learn, Teach

What you learn, teach.
What you get, give.

Maya Angelou (1928-),
African American writer/poet
Quoted by Humanitarian Award Winner Oprah Winfrey at Emmy Awards 2002

Stand Up, Be Counted: Teach What You Are

Your playing small doesn't serve the world. There is nothing enlightened about shrinking so that others will not feel insecure around you. We are born to manifest the glory of God that is within us. It is not just some of us, it is in everyone and as we let our own light shine, we unconsciously give people permission to do the same. As we are liberated from our own fear, our presence automatically liberates others.

Nelson Mandela (1918-),
South African political leader, liberator, writer
Speech

Evil

Philosophers, religious leaders, parents—everyone says don't do evil. But what is evil? Something in us? Something outside us? Is the evil of wars, torture, terrorism, starvation, due to ignorance, mental illness, human pathology? Or are there outside, universal forces for Good and Evil?

Is There a God Who Allows Evil?

If the suffering of children is the price of a ticket to heaven, then I respect-fully return my ticket.

> Fyodor Dostoyevsky (1821-1881),
> Russian psychological novelist
> *The Brothers Karamazov*, V, 4

Spit, and It Lands in Someone's Eye: Love, and Ditto

There is goodness and that which is called evil or bad, it exists in the world apart from our own contribu-tion to it...Either one contributes to goodness or to the so-called that which is bad.

> J. Krishnamurti,
> *Public Question & Answer Meeting,*
> *Aug. 30, 1984*

Is the Human Brain a Malign Tumor that Causes All Evil?

Nature is neutral. Man has wrested from nature the power to make the world a desert or to make the deserts bloom. There is no evil in the atom; only in men's souls.

> Adlai Stevenson (1900-1965),
> American political leader
> *Speech, Sept. 18, 1952*

We Know If We Do Good or Evil

Whoso has done an atom's weight of good shall see it; and whoso has done an atom's weight of evil shall see it.

> Mohammed, *Koran*, 99

The Evil We Do Always Hurts Somebody

When elephants fight it is the grass that suffers.

African Kikuyu Proverb

If You Live without Self-Concern, No Evil Can Hurt You Psychologically

No evil can happen to a good man, either in life or after death.

Plato, *Apology*, 41

If Evil Is Both In Us and Outside Us, What about Goodness?

What makes men good is held by some to be nature, by others habit or training, by others instruction. As for the goodness that comes by nature, this is plainly not within our control, but is bestowed by some divine agency on certain people who truly deserve to be called fortunate.

Aristotle (384-322 B.C.),
Greek philosopher
Nichomathean Ethics, X

Your Philosophy Here...

"Freedom's just another word for nothing left to lose. **"**

Kris Kristofferson, *Me and Bobby McGee*

Failure ——————————————————

Failure

Fear

Freedom

Friendship

Failure

[See also: Success]

There is no shame, no failure, without the arrogance of self-esteem. If we stopped being so self-important, we could also stop hating ourselves when we think we have failed.

Get off It

We all place ourselves at various levels, and we are constantly falling from these heights. It is the falls we are ashamed of. Self-esteem is the cause of our shame…If there is no pedestal on which you have put yourself, how can there be any fall?

J. Krishnamurti,
Commentaries on Living I, Ch. 5

If We Don't Set Ourselves Up as Experts, We Can't Fail

Great indeed is Confucius! He knows about everything, and is an expert at nothing.

Confucius, *The Wisdom of Confucius, Analects, III*

Do Your Best, Enjoy What You Do, Never Mind the Results

You have the right to work, but for the work's sake only. You have no right to the fruits of work. Desire for the fruits of work must never be your motive in working…Renounce attachment to the fruits. Be even-tempered in success and failure…They who work selfishly for results are miserable.

Krishna, *The Bhagavad-Gita, The Yoga of Knowledge*

FAILURE

Failure

Success Is Always Only Temporary Anyway

Those who would take over the earth
And shape it to their will
Never, I notice, succeed...
For a time in the world some force
    themselves ahead
And some are left behind,
For a time in the world some make a
    great noise
And some are held silent,
For a time in the world some are
    puffed fat
And some are kept hungry...
At no time in the world will a man
    who is sane
Over-reach himself,
Over-spend himself,
Over-rate himself.

Lao Tzu, The Way of Life, 29

Top of the Charts One Day, Gone the Next

Here lies one whose name was writ
in water.

John Keats (1795-1821),
English poet
Epitaph for Himself

It's the Life in Us that Is Immortal, Not What We Do

"My name is Ozymandias, king of
    kings:
Look on my works, ye mighty, and
    despair!"
Nothing beside remains. Round the
    decay
Of that colossal wreck, boundless
    and bare,
The lone and level sands stretch far
    away.

Percy Bysshe Shelley (1792-1822),
English poet, Ozymandias

About the Self-Importance of Worrying about Failure or Success

Go stand in a corner and count yourself—you're not so many.

Minnesota Farmwoman

Learning Is What's Important: Failures and Mistakes Don't Matter

"Murphy's Law": If anything can go
wrong, it will.

Saying, 1950's

Fear

Fear that is physical is really just the body's intelligence. You don't want to get hit by a truck. Psychological fear is the problem: it's based on thinking and time. What scares us is thinking the pain of yesterday will happen again tomorrow. You have to think about facts like traffic and where you next meal is coming from to stay alive. It's psychological thought that creates fear. Experiment: Stop thinking, just look at a tree or something outside yourself, and fear disappears.

We waste energy because we are all afraid of one thing or another all the time. We are all mostly interested in ourselves, in our lives, in our own reputations. What we are afraid of is not getting what we want or losing what we have. So we fear death, of the body, of our selves, of our egos. We fear losing popularity, the people and things we depend on, our friends, money, jobs, a place in the world. We fear darkness, loneliness, inner emptiness. We fear authority, certain people. One problem is that we are ashamed to admit our interest is 'me first', and so we never face our fears.

Fear Is a Great Teacher: Be Aware of Your Fears and Learn about Yourself

Fear is an extraordinary jewel, extraordinary something which has dominated human beings for forty thousand years and more. And if you can hold it and look at it, then one begins to see the ending of it...which means fear is part of our self-centered, egotistic activity. Fear is when the ego, the me, is isolated, when the me, the self, this self-centered movement because it is separative, because it is the very essence of conflict and all the rest of it, that is the root of fear.

J. Krishnamurti,
Public Talk 2, Brockwood Park, 1984

FEAR

Fear Is No Big Deal— Understand It and Move On

Questioner: I understand fear which is the memory and anticipation of pain. It is essential for the preservation of the organism…What puzzles me…[are] states of mind which have nothing to do with survival.

Nisargadatta: The personal self by its very nature is constantly pursuing pleasure and avoiding pain. The ending of this pattern is the ending of the self…with its desires and fears…It is this clash between desire and fear that causes anger, which is the great destroyer of sanity in life. When pain is accepted for what it is, a lesson and a warning, and deeply looked into and heeded, the separation between pain and pleasure breaks down, both become experience—painful when resisted, joyful when accepted.

Nisargadatta Maharaj,
I Am That, Ch. 59

We Are Never Taught How to Handle the Psychological Pain of Fear: Only How to Escape It into Sex, Work, Drugs and Alcohol, Making Money: Understanding Dissolves Fear with No Hangovers or Side Effects

We try so hard to overcome the separateness. More intimacy. More rubbing of bodies. More exchanging of ideas. But it's always as if you are yelling out of your room and I am yelling out of mine. Who am I? The room that the mind built.

We spend so much effort to get out of something that didn't exist until we created it.

Ram Dass (Richard Alpert),
The Journey of Awakening, Ch. 1

Fear Only Fear

The only thing we have to fear is fear itself.

> Franklin Delano Roosevelt
> (1882-1945), American president
> *First Inaugural Address 1933*

Stop Thinking about Yourself, and You Won't Be Afraid—It Is Your Own Imagination that Scares You—Turn Your Eyes into Windows, Not Mirrors

Such tricks hath strong imagination,
That, if it would but apprehend some
>joy,
It comprehends some bringer of that
>joy;
Or in the night, imagining some fear,
How easy is a bush supposed a bear!

> William Shakespeare, *A Midsummer—Night's Dream, V, i*

There Is Appropriate Fear

I am sorry to say that there is too much point to the wisecrack that life is extinct on other planets because their scientists were more advanced than ours.

> John F. Kennedy (1917-1963),
> American president
> *Speech, 1959*

FEAR

63

Freedom

Psychological freedom: do we really want it? Or just better security, more safety. In truth, the only real security is to learn to live without it. Dependency, whether on friends, lovers, parents, teachers, even old ideas, only creates fear of losing or doubting what you depend on, never freedom.

Might as Well Enjoy Standing on Our Own Two Feet: We Have to Anyway

It is very disappointing to realize that we must work on ourselves and our suffering rather than depend upon a savior…

> Chogyam Trungpa (1939-1987),
> Tibetan Buddhist philosopher,
> American teacher
> *The Myth of Freedom, Ch. I*

Since We Have to Stand Alone, We Better Learn How to Be Free Happily

All-pervading pain is the general pain of dissatisfaction, separation, and loneliness. We are alone, we are lonely people, we cannot regenerate our umbilical cord.

> Chogyam Trungpa,
> *The Myth of Freedom, Ch. 1*

We Are a Social Animal—We Must Live in the World among Family and Friends—Yet Mentally We Can Stand Alone

It is like living among snow-capped peaks with clouds wrapped around them and the sun and moon starkly shining over them…Aloneness becomes their companion, their spiritual consort, part of their being. Wherever they go they are alone, whatever they do they are alone. Whether they relate socially with friends or meditate alone…aloneness is there all the time. That aloneness is freedom, fundamental freedom.

> Chogyam Trungpa,
> *The Myth of Freedom, VII p*

If you Want to Be Free, Don't Depend

Freedom's just another word for nothing left to lose.

Kris Kristofferson (1936-),
American songwriter
Me and Bobby McGee, Country Song

Personal, Inner Freedom Must Be Learned; Political Freedom Must Be Provided

Preamble:

We the people of the United States, in order to form a more perfect Union, establish justice, insure domestic tranquillity, provide for the common defense, promote the general welfare, and secure the blessings of liberty to ourselves and our posterity do ordain and establish this Constitution for the United States of America.

First Amendment:

Congress shall make no law respecting an establishment of religion, or prohibiting the free exercise thereof; or abridging the freedom of speech, or of the press; or the right of the people peaceably to assemble.

Fourteenth Amendment

...nor shall any State deprive any person of life, liberty, or property, without due process of law...

Fifteenth Amendment

The right of citizens of the United States to vote shall not be denied or abridged...on account of race, color, or previous condition of servitude.

*The Constitution of the
United States,* 1787

FREEDOM

Any Slavery Makes Slaves of Us All

Where justice is denied, where poverty is enforced, where ignorance prevails, and where any one class is made to feel that society is in an organized conspiracy to oppress, rob, and degrade them, neither persons nor property will be safe.

Frederick Douglass (1818-1895), African American author/publisher *Speech in Washington, D. C. April 1885*

No man can put a chain about the ankle of his fellow man without at last finding the other fastened about his own neck.

Frederick Douglass, *Speech in Washington, D. C., October, 1883*

Two Slave Figures, Not One, Haunt Our History

So intense was the feeling, so mighty the human passions that swayed and blinded men. Amid it all, two figures ever stand to typify that day to coming ages, —the one, a gray-haired gentleman...who bowed to the evil of slavery...who stood at last, in the evening of life, a blighted, ruined form, with hate in his eyes; —and the other, a form hovering dark and motherlike, her awful face black with the mists of centuries, had aforetime quailed at that white master's command, had bent in love over the cradles of his sons and daughters, and...at his behest had laid herself low to his lust, and borne a tawny man-child to the world, only to see her dark boy's limbs scattered to the winds by midnight marauders riding after "cursed Niggers..." hating, they went to their long home, and, hating, their childrens' children live today.

Here, then, was the field of work for the Freedmen's Bureau.

William E. B. du Bois, *The Souls of Black Folk, II Of the Dawn of Freedom*

Give Us Freedom, or Give Us Death

We...would rather die on our feet than live on our knees.

Franklin Delano Roosevelt, *Speech, Oxford University, June 1941*

In Some Countries, the Freedom to Live Equally Is Subtracted According to Religion or Economic Class; In Others, Sex; In Others, Color

If you're born in America with a black skin, you're born in prison.

Malcolm X [El Hajj Malik El-Shabazz] (1925-1965), African American activist *Interview, June, 1963*

Only Idiots Think They Can Own a Piece of the Free Universe: We Are Just Caretakers

No tribe has the right to sell, even to each other, much less to strangers.... Sell a country! Why not sell the air, the great sea, as well as the earth? Didn't the Great Spirit make them all for the use of his children?

Tecumseh (1768-1813), Shawnee Warrior and Statesman *Speech*

Friendship

A quick measure of whether people are your friends is to note whether their faces generally look glad to see you. Simply put, a friend is friendly, affectionate, and treats you with respect. Friendship is equality: it isn't a license of ownership.

The friendship that can cease has never been real.

> St. Jerome (340?-420),
> *Panonian author of Vulgate,*
> *Latin version of the Bible, Letter 3*

The only way to have a friend is to be one.

> Ralph Waldo Emerson (1803-1882),
> American essayist
> *Essays: Friendship*

The best mirror is an old friend.

> George Herbert (1593-1633),
> English metaphysical poet
> *Jacula Prudentum*

He who has a thousand friends has not a friend to spare,

And he who has one enemy will meet him everywhere.

> Ali Ibn-Abu-Talib [Mohammed's
> Son-in-Law] (7th c.),
> Arabian poet
> *A Hundred Sayings*

He removes the greatest ornament of friendship, who takes away from it respect.

> Marcus Tullius Cicero
> (106-43 B.C.),
> Roman statesman/philosopher
> *De Amicita, XXII*

Hello darkness my old friend
I've come to talk with you again.
The words of the prophets
Are written on the subway walls
And tenement halls.
And whispered in the sounds of si-
lence.

Paul Simon (1942-),
American songwriter
The Sounds of Silence

Oh I'll get by with a little help from
my friends.

John Lennon (1940-1980),
British songwriter
*With a Little Help
from My Friends*

FRIENDSHIP

" Do what is good. Many do not know we are here in this world to live in harmony. Those who know this, do not fight against each other. **"**

Buddha, *The Dhammapada*

God ⎯⎯⎯⎯⎯⎯⎯⎯⎯⎯⎯⎯⎯⎯⎯⎯⎯⎯⎯⎯

God

God

Is there God? Go outside and look at a tree. If no human brain you know of can create one, there is probably God. Mostly when people argue about God, they are arguing over the word 'God' and what the word means according to some system they have been taught. It seems perfectly clear to most philosophers and scientists that some intelligence, some force, something that certainly is not a human being created atoms, space, and makes life out of a few chemicals.

God/Goddess Has Thousands of Faces in India, Africa, China, Japan, Just as Among the Greeks, Romans, and Nordic Peoples of Europe

There was always too much work for one god.

Edgar M. Bick, M. D. (1902-1978),
American orthopedic
surgeon/philosopher
Letter to His Daughter, 1957

God/Goddess Has Thousands of Names in the West

Religious scholars have related that Allah has three thousand Names. One thousand are only known by angels, 1, 000 known only by prophets, 300 are in the Torah (Old Testament), 300 are in Zabur (Psalms of David), 300 are in the New Testament, and 99 are in the Qu'ran. This makes 2, 999 Names. One Name which has been hidden by Allah is called Ism Allah al-a'zam: The Greatest Name of Allah.

Shems Friedlander, with al-Hajj
Shaikh Muzaffereddin
(1916-) Arabic philosopher
*Ninety-Nine Names of Allah,
Foreword*

GOD

God

The English word for god has the same base as the word 'good.' See any dictionary.

Humans Argue Details, but They All Sense Powers Greater Than Their Own

In the West, mystics generally regard the universe as real and God as personal, while most Eastern traditions regard God as impersonal and the universe as illusory.

Holmes Welch (20th c.),
American philosopher
Taoism: The Parting of the Way, 3

The Mind of God

...if we do discover a complete [unified] theory [of the universe], it should be understandable in broad principle by everyone, not just a few scientists. Then we shall all, philosophers, scientists, and just ordinary people, be able to take part in the discussion of the question of why it is that we and the universe exist. If we find the answer to that, it would be the ultimate triumph of human reason—for then we would know the mind of God.

Stephen Hawking, *A Brief History of Time*, Ch. 11

Buddha Said Simply—Behave, Live Rightly, and You Are Already with God

Do not what is evil. Do what is good.

Buddha, *The Dhammapada*

God Cannot Be Organized as Religions Can—You Have to Make the Phone Call Yourself—Just Be Absolutely Silent, and the Connection Occurs

It is in the moments of Being when [humans have] found THAT beyond words and thought and [have] called it Brahman, Atman, Elohim, God, Nirvana, Tao, Allah, or OM which according to the Upanishads includes all names, and other sacred words.

In a state of contemplation and union the knower and the known are one.

Juan Mascaro (d. 1987),
Majorcan professor/
translator/philosopher
The Dhammapada: The Path of Perfection, Introduction

Leave Yourself Out of It, and God Is There

Being out in nature with no other thoughts is like kissing God.

Hannah Carlson (1963-),
American psychotherapist
The Courage to Lead: Start Your Own Support Group—Mental Illnesses and Addictions

We've All Had Moments with God, the Spirit of the Universe, by Whatever Name You Call WHAT Is Beyond, Behind, Eternal

A moment. The moment of orgasm. The moment by the ocean when there is just the wave. The moment of being in love. The moment of crisis when we forget ourselves and do just what is needed...

These moments appear again and again in our lives...This glimpse reveals to the person that there is something more...when you "forget yourself. "

Ram Dass (Richard Alpert),
*The Journey of Awakening,
Introduction*

" Do you think happiness is an end in itself? Or does it come as a secondary thing in living intelligently?...what is important is not happiness, but whether unhappiness can end. **"**

J. Krishnamurti, *The Urgency of Change*

Happiness ─────────────────

Happiness

Hate

Happiness

We look for happiness in things and relationships, in pleasures like sex, food, drugs, shopping. But these don't last longer than a flash of lightning. The happiness that goes on and on is actually a by-product of living so that the brain is full of living itself, not 'me' and what the 'me' wants.

Stop the Pain, and Happiness Is

Do you think happiness is an end in itself? Or does it come as a secondary thing in living intelligently?… what is important is not happiness, but whether unhappiness can end…Can an outside agency help you to get rid of your own misery, whether that outside agency be God, a master, a drug, or a savior? Or can one have the intelligence to understand the nature of unhappiness and deal with it immediately?

J. Krishnamurti,
The Urgency of Change, Happiness

Unmake Misery to Make Happiness

The two foes of human happiness are pain and boredom.

Arthur Schopenhauer (1788-1860),
German philosopher
Essays

Happiness Is Going with the Flow

In spite of illness, in spite even of the archenemy sorrow, one can remain alive…if one is unafraid of change, insatiable in intellectual curiosity, interested in big things, and happy in small ways.

Edith Wharton (1862-1937),
American novelist
A Backward Glance, A First Word

Happiness

We Better Be Happy

...where happiness fails, existence remains a mad and lamentable experiment.

George Santayana (1863-1952),
American philosopher
The Life of Reason, Vol I

If Happiness Is Too Heavy for You

There are moments when everything goes well; don't be frightened, it won't last.

Jules Renard (1864-1910),
French philosopher
Journal

What Doesn't Make You Happy?

Hell is—other people!

Jean Paul Sartre (1905-1980),
French writer/philosopher
No Exit, sc. v

What Does?

Happiness is a warm puppy.

Charles Schulz (1922-),
American cartoonist
Happiness Is a Warm Puppy

Hate

In the Western world, we have the habit of thinking in opposite pairs of ideas. In fact, hate is not the opposite of love. Hate has nothing to do with love. Like evil, hate is a horror all its own. It seems to have its root in fear and anger: it is often conditioned by cultures for generations, or by the media. It can be organized in peer groups, this gang hating that gang, teens hating parents, this country hating that country. It can be personal: hurt feelings organizing themselves into hateful rage.

You Have to Be Taught to Hate

You have to be taught to hate and
    fear,
It has to be drummed in your dear
    little ear.
You have to be carefully taught.

> Oscar Hammerstein (1895-1960),
> American playwright/songwriter
> *South Pacific*

Customs Dictate Your Feelings: However, You Have the Power to See This and Change Them

From the moment of his birth, the customs into which [an individual] is born shape his experience and behavior. By the time he can talk, he is the little creature of his culture.

> Ruth Benedict (1887-1948),
> American sociologist
> *Patterns of Culture, Ch. 1*

Self-Hate Is Also Taught, by Comparisons, Put-Downs: It Is Very Catching

Does it matter whether you hate
    your...self?
At least
Love your eyes that can see, your
    mind that can
Hear the music, the thunder of the
    wings. Love the wild swan.

> Robinson Jeffers (1887-1962),
> American poet
> *Love the Wild Swan*

Hate Is Just Fear

Whom they fear they hate.

> Quintus Ennius (239-169 B.C.),
> Roman philosopher
> *Cicero, 11, 7*

"The life which is unexamined is not worth living. "

Socrates, *Apology*

Intellect and Intelligence:
Information and Insight

Intellect and Intelligence,

Insight and Information

Intellect and Intelligence: Information and Insight

Intellect and information are memory, accumulated past knowledge. Insight, intelligence, perception, understanding, these are not to be found in books, only in living with attention to your insides and outsides every moment.

Don't Confuse Good Marks with a Good Mind

Training the intellect does not result in intelligence. Rather, intelligence comes into being when one acts in perfect harmony, both intellectually and emotionally. There is a vast distinction between intellect and intelligence. Intellect is merely thought functioning.

Until you really approach all of life with your intelligence, instead of merely with your intellect, no system in the world will save man from the ceaseless toil for bread.

J. Krishnamurti,
What Are You Doing With Your Life?—Books on Living for Teens, Ch. 4

Intellect Earns You a Living: Only Intelligence Will Tell You What to Do with It

The life which is unexamined is not worth living.

Socrates, *Apology*, 38

Perception

Imagination [perceptive insight] is more important than knowledge. Knowledge is limited; imagination circles the world.

Albert Einstein
Science Says, ed. Rob Kaplan

INTELLECT AND INTELLIGENCE

85

Intellect and Intelligence: Information and Insight

INTELLECT AND INTELLIGENCE

Insight

A moment's insight is sometimes worth a life's experience.

> Oliver Wendell Holmes, Sr.
> (1809-1894), American writer
> *The Professor at the Breakfast Table*

Understanding

...making your ear attentive to wisdom
and inclining your heart to understanding;
yes, if you cry out for insight
and raise your voice for understanding,
if you seek it like silver
and search for it as for hidden treasures
then you will understand...
and find the knowledge of God.

> Solomon, King of Israel (ca. 973-933
> B.C.), philosopher/lawgiver
> *Bible, Old Testament, Proverbs, 2*

Watchfulness Is Paying Attention

And he came to the disciples and found them sleeping; and he said to Peter, "So you could not watch with me one hour?...the spirit indeed is willing, but the flesh is weak. "

> Jesus of Nazareth,
> *Bible, New Testament, Matthew 2*

Inattention Is Not Only Dumb, but Dangerous

...who has the joy of watchfulness and who looks with fear on thoughtlessness, he goes on his path like a fire, burning all obstacles both great and small.

> Buddha, *The Dhammapada, 2*

86

Loving Attention to Life Is Intelligence

When people lost sight of the way to
live
Came codes of love and honesty,
Learning came, charity came,
Hypocrisy took charge...
Rid of formalized wisdom and learn-
ing
People would be a hundredfold hap-
pier,
Rid of conventionalized duty and
honor
People would find their families
dear...

Lao Tzu, *The Way of Life, 18-19*

Knowledge Is Just the Endless Accumulation of Facts: The Intelligence of Insight Occurs in a Minute

"Opening one's eyes may take a life-
time. Seeing is done in a flash. "

Anthony de Mello (1931-1987),
American spiritual philosopher
One Minute Wisdom, 1

To Change Human History, Its Suffering and Terrors, We Need, Not More Intellectual Technology, but a Whole New Approach

...a new creative surge [is] called for
in order to meet the extraordinary
challenge that is now facing the human race...The essence of the
creative act is a state of high energy
making possible a fresh perception,
generally through the mind...that
cannot be limited or grasped in any
definable form of knowledge or skill.

David Bohm,
Science, Order, and Creativity,
Summary and Outlook

Without Attentive Observation, What you see Is What You Are

Every man takes the limits of his own
field of vision for the limits of the
world.

Arthur Schopenhauer,
Studies in Pessimism, Psychological
Observations

INTELLECT AND
INTELLIGENCE

87

66 Lord, grant that I may seek rather to comfort than be comforted—to understand rather than to be understood…. 77

St. Francis, *Prayer*

Jealousy

Jealousy

Joy

Justice: Fairness

Jealousy

Jealousy is dependency, possession, fear of abandonment, losing face, pride, not love.

Has Jealousy Anything to Do with Loving Someone?

In jealousy there is more self-love than love.

Francois, Duc de La Rochefoucauld (1630-1680),
French philosopher
Reflections; or, Sentences and Moral Maxims

Jealousy Is Anger, Not Love

Jealousy feeds upon suspicion, and it turns into fury or it ends as soon as we pass from suspicion to certainty.

La Rochefoucauld, *Maxim 32*

Love Is Strength, Jealousy Its Absence

...love is strong as death; jealousy is cruel as the grave.

King Solomon, *Bible, Song of Solomon, 8: 6*

Othello Killed His Wife Desdemona Not for Love, but Jealousy

O! beware, my lord, of jealousy,
It is the green-ey'd monster which
    doth mock
The meat it feeds on...

Shakespeare, *Othello, III, iii*

Love Has No Opposite

Have you really loved someone if, when they leave you for someone else, you stop loving them?

Ray Fisher, *Unpublished Works*

JEALOUSY

Joy

Joy does not depend on anything outside you the way pleasure does. Joy is an inner response to something: to a beautiful sky, connection to the universe or another human being, just to being alive. Joy happens in moments free of fear and self-preoccupation.

Joy Cannot Be Hunted: It Happens When We Aren't Looking

We are constantly seeking new excitements, new thrills, we crave an ever-increasing variety of sensations... There is lasting joy only when we are capable of approaching all things fresh—which is not possible as long as we are bound up in our desires.

J. Krishnamurti,
Education and the Significance of Life, VIII

Repeated Pleasure Becomes Boring: Joy Is Experiencing Everything as If It Were the First Time

I cannot cause light; the most I can do is try to put myself in the path of its beam. It is possible in deep space to sail on solar wind...Hone and spread your spirit till you yourself are a sail...broadside to the merest puff.

Annie Dillard (1945-),
American writer
Pilgrim at Tinker Creek, Ch. 2

3333

33333333

Isn't There Joy in the Razor-Sharp Understanding of Connection, an Instant of Insight, the Discovery of Truth?

The nineteenth century was the first century of human sympathy, —the age when half wonderingly we began to descry in others that transfigured spark of divinity which we call Myself; when clodhopper and peasants, and tramps and thieves, and millionaires and sometimes Negroes, became throbbing souls whose warm pulsing life touched us so nearly that we half gasped with surprise, crying, "Thou too! Hast Thou seen Sorrow and the dull waters of Hopelessness? Hast Thou known Life?" And then all helplessly we peered into those Other-worlds and wailed, "O World of Worlds, how shall man make you one?"

W. E. B. du Bois, *The Souls of Black Folk, Ch. XII*

Joy Happens When the Self Is Absent and Life Occurs

These moments are ones in which we have "lost ourselves, "or been "taken out of ourselves," or "forgotten ourselves." They are moments in flow. …there is no longer separation. There is peace, harmony, tranquillity, the joy of being part of the process. In these moments the universe appears fresh; it is seen through innocent eyes. It all begins anew.

Ram Dass, *The Journey of Awakening, Ch. 1*

Justice: Fairness

Life isn't fair. Some of us are born gorgeous, some not. Some of us are born smart, some not so smart; some healthy, some with physical or mental problems; some into places where people eat every day, some into hunger. We discover young, usually in our early teens, that tornadoes or sunny days, whether some people get caught cheating or they don't, happen due to millions of causes and effects, not because there is justice. What we call luck is that we can't see or calculate all the odds.

We Only Sense Fairness and Justice When Things Go Our Way

The collisions begin in earliest infancy, with the discovery that the sources of our satisfaction lie beyond our control and that the world does not reliably conform to our desires.

Alain de Botton (1969-),
French philosopher
*Seneca, Consolations
of Philosophy, Ch. 3*

Our Expectations Are the Basis for Our Frustrations

We aren't overwhelmed by anger whenever we are denied an object we desire, only when we believe ourselves entitled to obtain it. Our greatest furies spring from events which violate our sense of the ground rules of existence.

Seneca,
*Consolations of Philosophy,
Ch. 3*, Alain de Botton

94

There Is a Problem with Justice

One man's justice is another's injustice.

Ralph Waldo Emerson (1803-1873),
American philosopher
Essays, First Series

Because People Do Not Deal with Each Other Justly, We Make Legal Promises

I pledge allegiance to my [the] flag [of the United States of America] and to the republic for which it stands, one nation [under God], indivisible, with liberty and justice for all.

Francis Bellamy (1856-1931),
American patriot
The Pledge of Allegiance to the Flag, 1892 [bracketed words written in later]

Part of the Problem Is We Are Told There Is Justice Early in Life

A feeling that the rules of justice have been violated, rules which dictate that if we are honorable, we will be rewarded, and that if we are bad, we will be punished—a sense of justice [is] inculcated in the earliest education of children, and found in most religious texts.

Seneca,
Consolations of Philosophy, Ch. 3,
Alain de Botton

JUSTICE:
FAIRNESS

What Saves Us from Self-Hate, Self-Centered Fear, Rage at What Isn't Fair, May Be to Remember It Isn't All About Us

But we cannot always explain our destiny by referring to our moral worth; we may be cursed and blessed without justice behind either. Not everything which happens to us occurs with reference to something about us.

Seneca,
Consolations of Philosophy, Ch. 3,
Alain de Botton

Historically, We All Live in Glass Houses—Be Careful about Throwing Stones

A thought that haunts many African Americans I know is that they are the same distance from the slave owner as from the slave. Both strains have contributed to their bodies, to their waking spirits. I am the same distance from the conquistador as from the Indian. Righteousness should not come easily to any of us...

Our irreducible element is not "I," as it turns out, but some ghostly "we," cumulative, remote instructions that can be traced across the plains of Africa, all the way back to the finger of God.

Richard Rodriguez (1944-),
American essayist
*Brown: the Last Discovery
of America, Ch. 9*

Your Philosophy Here...

" I think the person who has had more experience of hardships can stand more firmly in the face of problems than the person who has never experienced suffering. "

Dalai Lama, *Book of Wisdom*

Killing

Killing

Knowledge

Killing

Killing Hurts the Killer

If you look at the living process closely, you will find cruelty everywhere, for life feeds on life...To the last day of your life you will compete for food, clothing, shelter, holding on to your body, fighting for its needs, wanting it to be secure, in a world of insecurity and death. From the animal's point of view being killed is not the worst form of dying; surely preferable to sickness and senile decay. The cruelty lies in the motive, not in the fact. Killing hurts the killer, not the killed.

Nisargadatta Maharaj,
I Am That, Ch. 36

There Are Many Forms of Killing—Being Vegetarian Isn't All There Is To It

There are many forms of killing, are there not? There is killing by a word or gestures, killing in fear or in anger, killing for a country or an ideology, killing for a set of economic dogmas or religious beliefs...

With a word or gesture you kill a man's reputation...And does not comparison kill? Don't you kill a boy by comparing him with another who is cleverer or more skillful? A man who kills out of hate or anger is regarded as a criminal and put to death. Yet the man who deliberately bombs thousands of people off the face of the earth in the name of his country is honored, decorated; he is looked upon as a hero...Animals are killed for food, for profit, or for so-called sport; they are vivisected for the well-being of man...

So, the issue we are discussing is not merely the killing or the nonkilling

KILLING

101

of animals, but the cruelty and hate that are ever increasing in the world and in each one of us. That is our real problem, isn't it?

> J. Krishnamurti,
> *Commentaries on Living*, III, Ch. 32

What You Do Is What You Become

Let every soul look upon the morrow for the deed it has performed.

> Mohammed, *The Koran*, 59: 18

Are Heroes Really People Who Kill?

When John F. Kennedy was assassinated, Malcolm X said: "It was, as I saw it, a case of 'the chicken coming home to roost. ' I said that the hate in white men had not stopped with the killing of defenseless black people, but that hate, allowed to spread unchecked, had finally struck down this country's Chief Magistrate."

> Malcolm X {El Hajj Malik El Shabazz], *Autobiography*

Revolution Is Psychological, not Killing People

You say you want a revolution
Well you know
we all want to change the world...
But when you talk about destruction
Don't you know that you can count
me out.

> John Lennon (1940-1980) and Paul
> McCartney (1942-),
> English songwriters
> *Revolution*

Killing Is not Safe for Children

He had grown up in a country run by politicians who sent the pilots to man the bombers to kill the babies to make the world safer for children to grow up in.

> Ursula Kroeber Le Guin (1929-),
> American writer
> *The Lathe of Heaven*, Ch. 6

Knowledge

About Relationship to People: Image-Forming Prevents Seeing

Knowledge and experience are physically necessary to find food, your way back to your cave, and to remember that a lion will eat you and a tree will not. Psychologically, in relationship, knowledge and experience create images of people that just get in the way of really seeing them. Knowledge and experience, thoughts, which are the records the brain keeps of everything, tells you only the past, the long past of thousands of generations—or yesterday. Only a fresh look in the present moment can tell you how to behave in the present moment.

About Things: Technology and Vision

We are taught science and other forms of knowledge in fragments, in separate disciplines. We are not taught the overview: the intelligent use of knowledge. Our brains are flexible enough for both capacities: knowledge and its intelligent use.

We Are Not Just Biologically Determined: We Have Biological Potential

Human uniqueness lies in the flexibility of what our brain can do. What is intelligence, if not the ability to face problems in an unprogrammed (or, as we often say, creative) manner?... What would be more adaptive for a learning and thinking animal: genes selected for aggression, spite, and xenophobia; or selection for learning rules that can generate aggression in appropriate circumstances and peacefulness in others?

Stephen Jay Gould, *The Mismeasure of Man*, Ch. 7

KNOWLEDGE

Knowledge

We Make Profit, not Human Well-Being, a Priority

If the human race wants to go to hell in a basket, technology can help it get there by jet.

Charles M. Allen (1939-),
American science philosopher
Speech, Winston-Salem, N. C.

A Chemistry Set Can Plunge the World into Darkness: High Tech Isn't Even Necessary, Only an Inhuman Lack of Ethics

Concern for man and his fate must always form the chief interest of all technical endeavors…in order that the creations of our mind shall be a blessing and not a curse to mankind. Never forget this in the midst of your diagrams and equations.

Why does this magnificent applied science which saves work and makes life easier bring us so little happiness? The simple answer runs: Because we have not yet learned to make sensible use of it.

Albert Einstein, *Speech, Pasadena, from Science Says*, Rob Kaplan

Used Rightly, Knowledge Serves Well

It is science alone that can solve the problems of hunger and poverty, in-sanitation and illiteracy, of superstition and deadening custom and tradition, of vast resources running to waste, of a rich country inhabited by starving people…. The future belongs to science and to those who make friends with science.

Jawaharlal Nehru (1889-1964),
Indian statesman and political
philosopher, *Speech, National
Institute of Sciences, India*

What Are the Proper Uses of Science?

Why does not science, instead of troubling itself about sunspots, which nobody ever saw, or, if they did, ought not to speak about; why does not science busy itself with drainage and sanitary engineering? Why does it not clean the streets and free the rivers from pollution?

Oscar Wilde (1834-1900),
English writer, wit, philosopher
*Oscar Wilde: Interviews and
Recollections*

We Divide Knowledge Into Compartments Instead of Seeing the Whole Picture

In science education, developing the scientific spirit is far more important than to cram the brain with the details of information. The scientific spirit is the spirit of precision, accuracy, and efficiency, not personal or national idiosyncrasy...emphasis needs to be given to the arts of observation, experimentation, and learning for oneself. And once developed, these arts, this same independent spirit can be applied to learning about the inward life as well as the outer world. In this way, the spirit of science and the spirit of religious compassion become one. This is far more important than the mere discovery of yet more scientific facts, lest these be used only for self-centered purposes.

Kishore Khairnar (1954-),
Indian physicist/philosopher
In and Out of Your Mind: Teen Science, Human Bites,
Dale Carlson

What Do We Really Want to Know?

...if science has scrutinized human consciousness only recently and leaves other disciplines, if any, to study human thought—then science, which is, God knows, correct, nevertheless cannot address what interests us most: What are we doing here?

Annie Dillard, *For the Time Being*

KNOWLEDGE

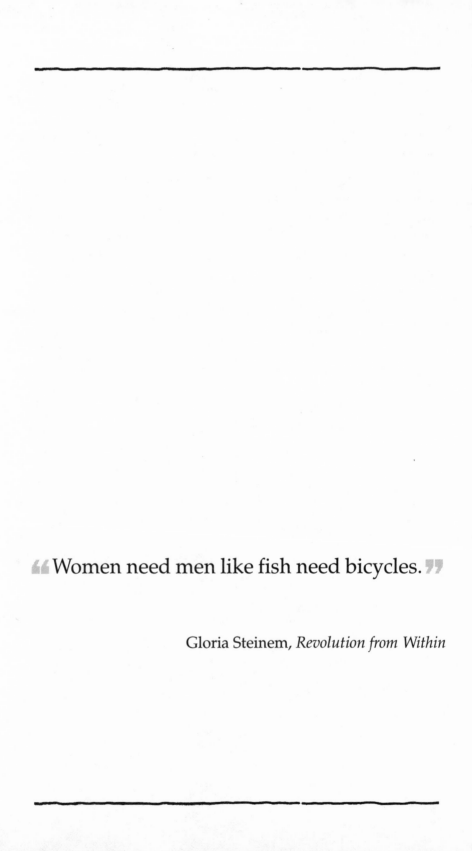

"Women need men like fish need bicycles.**"**

Gloria Steinem, *Revolution from Within*

Love

Loneliness

See: Depression

Love

Love

We use the word 'love' for everything from pizza to romance. And romantic love in our culture is a form of craziness, if you listen to our songs. It's a sort of neurotic disturbance—a compound of sex, biology, loneliness, the need for security, a passion for possession and power, dependency in a relabeled need for parenting, and a form of addiction to another person with desperate highs and equally desperate withdrawals, and an inability to stand on one's own two feet. Romantic love seems to describe a lostness that requires drama, and a part in an endless movie script—or at least a few hours' attention. And all of this is what we call 'being in love.'

Those with an extra scrap of intelligence and humor see through it at least long enough to suspect they are simply rationalizing the rollercoaster of chemistry.

Society Dresses Up the Word 'Love' to Reproduce Itself and to Control Our Lives

Forms of slavery in marriage are not far to seek. The husband bitterly bound to the responsibilities of making money, the wife determinedly sacrificing her gifts and talents... bound by guilt, by what their parents thought about marriage...As slaves do, they take their pain out on one another, playing deathly games in which selfishness, anger, and hate are dressed up to look like unselfishness, patience, and love...We can only set ourselves free from such sickness by going deeply enough into ourselves to find the courage to see what we are...[then] it will be possible for our marriage partners, or anyone else, to relate properly to us.

Monica Furlong (1930-),
English writer
*Ordinary Magic: Everyday
Life as Spiritual Path,*
ed. John Welwood, Ch. 32

Romance Is Fine: Just Call It Right and Don't Confuse It with Love

If we weren't so needy, so full of illusions about a magic rescue, so hooked on trying to own someone— in other words, if the conscious goal of romance were stretching our understanding of ourselves and others...romance could be a deep, intimate, sensual, empathetic way of learning: of seeing through someone else's eyes, feeling with their nerve endings, absorbing another culture or way of life from the inside, stretching our boundaries.

Gloria Steinem (1934-),
American feminist/philosopher/
writer/publisher
Revolution from Within,
Romance versus Love, II

Isn't Intimacy Possible Only Where There Is Equality and Respect? Laws Help, but You Can't Legislate Attitude

How can we change the conditions we have today?...[It is] clear that this family structure, designed to produce the gender stereotyping we have so long experienced, denies to men and women any real sense of each other as the object of profound intimacy. Men define themselves by their separation from women; women define themselves by their lack of separation...In the absence of those special factors that produce achieving women, they will cling to the male as husband and, in that role, as the definer of their identity.

Carolyn Heilbrun (1926-),
American writer
Reinventing Womanhood, Marriage
and Family, Ch. 6

Do Men and Women Really Love, Do Parents Really Love Their Children, Do We Really Love the Land? Why Then Is There War in Families, the World?

...Love cannot be divided into divine and physical; it is only love—not that you love many or the one...Love is not a memory. Love is not a thing of the mind or the intellect. But it comes into being naturally as compassion, when the whole problem of existence—as fear, greed, envy, despair, hope—has been understood and resolved. An ambitious man cannot love. A man who is attached to his family has no love. Nor has jealousy anything to do with love. When you say, "I love my wife," you really do not mean it, because the next moment you are jealous of her...

Love implies great freedom—not to do what you like. But love comes only when the mind is...not self-centered...If you have no love, do what you will—go after all the gods on earth, do all the social activities, try to reform the poor, the politics, write books, write poems—you are a dead human being.

J. Krishnamurti,
The Book of Life,
edited by R. E. Mark Lee

LOVE

111

"Then in the marriage union, the independence of husband and wife will be equal, their dependence mutual, and their obligations reciprocal. "

Lucretia Mott, *Discourse on Women*

Marriage

Marriage

Meditation: Mind: Silence

Money

See: Work

Marriage

[See also: Sex (married, single, heterosexual, homosexual)]

Only recently, as human history goes, marriage got confused with romance, sexual pleasure, and the general chaos of unmatured psychological needs, particularly the need to escape the loneliness caused by not understanding what our own feeling of emptiness is all about —not a lack of love, but a lack of loving! But at least now, for the most part, unlike the arranged marriages of most older civilizations, marriage is the legal decision of two people to join their journey through life, for companionship, and to raise children.

Most Religions Endorse Marriage—and Remarriage— Not Only as a Structure for Raising Children, but as a Safe and Proper Place for Sex

I would [even] have younger widows marry.

St. Paul, *Bible New Testament, I Timothy*, 5: 14

Some Religions Suggest Choosing Your Partner

Let them marry whom they think best.

Moses, *Bible, Old Testament, Numbers* 36: 6

Some Say It Is Better to Marry than to Obsess About Sex

The abstinent run away from what
    they desire
But carry their desires with them.

Krishna, *The Bhagavad-Gita*, *Yoga of Knowledge*

Some Religious People Really Approve of Marriage

There is no more lovely, friendly and charming relationship, communion or company than a good marriage.

Martin Luther (1483-1546), German religious leader and philosopher
On Marriage, 1530

115

True Marriage Can Only Be Between Equals: It Neither Exploits Women as Servants Nor Makes Men Carry the Whole Provider Burden

Let woman then go on—not asking favors, but claiming as a right the removal of all hindrances to her elevation in the scale of being—let her receive encouragement for the proper cultivation of all her powers, so that she may enter profitably into the active business of life...Then in the marriage union, the independence of the husband and wife will be equal, their dependence mutual, and their obligations reciprocal.

Lucretia Mott (1730-1880),
American co-founder,
first women's rights convention
Discourse on Women

We Are Human First, Gendered Second

When I went back to Park Slope, Brooklyn, where I came from, it was still a family neighborhood, people pushing baby carriages and swings. Only now the parents are lesbian and gay couples.

Harvey Fierstein (1954-) American
playwright/activist
In the Life, Speech

No Need to Marry

Some of us are becoming the men we wanted to marry.

*Gloria Steinem, Yale University
Speech*

A Good Marriage

Marriages dedicated to something greater than themselves seem to work better than those that merely feed on themselves.

R. E. Mark Lee (1940-), American
philosopher/teacher/editor
The Book of Life by
J. Krishnamurti, *Letter*

MARRIAGE

Meditation: Mind, Silence

Meditation comes from the Latin for 'attention'. It does not mean standing on your head making strange sounds. Meditation happens when thought stops. Thinking goes on all the time in the human brain. Attention to, not arguing with, those thoughts will give you insight into what's going on with you and what to do about it. Insight is now. You can always have insight. It is always now.

Meditation Is Not Self-Hypnosis

Not to seek any form of psychological security...requires investigation ...watchfulness to see how the mind operates, and surely that is meditation, is it not? Meditation is not the practice of a formula or the repetition of certain words, which is all silly, immature. Without knowing the whole process of the mind, conscious as well as unconscious, any form of meditation...is a form of self-hypnosis. But...discover for oneself the ways of the self—that is meditation. It is only through self-knowledge that the mind can be free to discover what is truth, what is God, what is death, what is this thing we call living.

J. Krishnamurti,
What Are You Doing With Your Life?
Books on Living for Teens Ch. 8

There Are Many Meditative Practices to Quiet the Brain's Chatter So Meditation Can Take Place—Sitting, Counting Breath, Walking, Reading, Singing, Dancing, Chanting, Praying

It helps to use a method which uses your natural tendencies...

Look at your life and see what has really turned you on. Perhaps you are very athletic. To sit motionless for an hour would be to fight your body. Instead you might begin with karate or kung fu and then go on to tai chi or some other moving meditation. If you are more sedentary or scholarly you might start by reading Krishnamurti or Buddhist doctrine, the Bible, Koran, Vedas, I Ching, Lao Tzu, Native American wisdom and practicing vipassana (yoga breathing) meditation. An emotional

117

person might...be drawn to Sufi dancing or to singing or chanting. These are also forms of meditation... Stop...sit comfortably...don't hold onto any...thoughts, but just let them keep flowing by; you are already in the act of meditation.

Ram Dass,
The Journey of Awakening, Ch. 3

Meditation Is Not Rules: It Is Mindfulness of What You Are Doing, Thinking, Feeling in Each Moment—Its Point Is So You Respond, Behave Appropriately, not Just React—Its Point Is So You Are Not In Your Own Way, So You Can Connect Lovingly with People, with the Universe

For everything there is a season, and time for every matter...a time to be born, and a time to die; ...a time to keep silence, and a time to speak...

The Preacher in *Ecclesiastes 3: 17*
Bible, Old Testament

True Meditation

Every move is a prayer.

Crow Dog Man (19th c.)
Crow Tribe

Meditation Is the Presence of God

We must be empty [of ourselves] if we want God to fill us.

Mother Teresa

Meditation Is the Absence of Pain

The basic fact is that all sentient beings, particularly human beings, want happiness and do not want pain and suffering. On those grounds, we have every right to be happy and to use different methods or means to overcome suffering and achieve happier lives.

Dalai Lama, *Dalai Lama's Book of Wisdom, p. 3*

Meditation Is the Absence of the Thinker

Meditation is not just about creating states of well-being: it is about destroying the belief in an inherently existent self...Insight arises when the thinker's existence is no longer necessary.

Mark Epstein, M. D.
Thoughts without a Thinker

Meditative Attention Is Necessary to See the Truthful Reality of Things—in Life as Well as in Science

Neither self nor things are continuously existent...All of them resemble successively lit bulbs in the skysign or the successively explicated states we interpret as particles...it is rather hard to assert that there is...a category called 'real' which is wholly uncompromised by the observing mind.

Alex Comfort, M. D., D. Sc. (1920-),
Reality and Empathy: Physics, Mind, and Science in the 21st Century, Intro.

Meditative Prayer: to Be Empty Rather than Full of Self

Lord, make me a channel of thy peace...grant that I may seek rather to comfort than to be comforted, to understand, than to be understood, to love, than to be loved. For it is by self-forgetting that one finds.

Francis of Assisi (c. 1181-1226),
Italian preacher/saint/ philosopher
Prayer

Turn on the Light in Your Brain: If Even One Person Has the Light on, Everyone Can See

You are the light of the world.

Jesus of Nazareth, *Bible, New Testament, Matthew 5: 14*

In the Silence of Meditation

Let go of the things in which you are in doubt for the things in which there is no doubt.

Mohammed, *The Koran*

" A walk in the rainforest is a walk into the mind of God. **"**

Birute Galdikas, *Reflections of Eden*

Nature

Nature

Nature

Go somewhere and look at the clouds, the trees, nature. We're so full of thoughts, ideas, opinions, we miss our whole relationship to it all. We forget that the grass, and the rabbits, and we are all made of the same atoms, out of stardust. Our loneliness and feelings of isolation are just an attitude, an illusion of separation, not a fact.

Physics and Ecology Tell Us the Same Thing

All things are connected. Whatever befalls the earth, befalls the children of the earth.

Chief Seattle, Squamish Tribe, *Speech, 1853*

Animals Are as Important to Each Other as Humans—They Are Not Ours to Own, Eat, Experiment On

Animals are other nations…
What is man without the beasts? If all the beasts were gone, men would die from great loneliness of spirit, for whatever happens to the beasts also happens to man. All things are connected.

Chief Seattle, *Speech, 1853*

Technological Humanity Is Not so Superior—We Have Actually Less Knowledge of Nature than Our Hunter-Gatherer Forebears

The whites, too, shall pass—perhaps sooner than other tribes. Continue to contaminate your own bed, and you will one night suffocate in your own waste.

Chief Seattle, *Speech*

NATURE

Nature

The Farther Away from Nature, the Fewer Our Natural Senses We Still Have

Telepathy is a normal form of communication among the Australian Aborigines. They've been around for 45, 000 years.

National Geographic
Explorer TV Series

We Are Not Even at the Top of the Information-Storage Chain

Elephants can store information better than humans can, based on the convolutions of the temporal lobes.

National Geographic
Explorer TV Series

Nature, Science, and Religion Are Fundamentally the Same Thing

The laws of nature are but the mathematical thoughts of God.

Euclid (c. 300 B.C.) Greek
mathematician/philosopher
Elements

It Is All God

A walk in the rainforest is a walk into the mind of God.

Birute Galdikas, Ph.D. (1946-),
Canadian/American primatologist
Reflections of Eden

Your Philosophy Here...

“ He [she] who is useful is infinite. **”**

Lao Tzu, *The Way of Life*

Parents and Family ———————

Parents and Family

Passion

Pleasure: Fun, Entertainment, Escape

Popularity: Power: Status

Purpose of Life

Parents and Family

Family must be loving relationship to all human existence, not an enclosed system that is exclusive, separative, and divisive like nations, religions, and tribes. If a family behaves like a tank, enclosing a few against the many, with its attitudes ready to shoot down, hate, fear, feel superior to or suspicious of—or even just exclude nonfamily— there is no love in this, only war. Neighborhoods are the outgrowth of family; tribes and nations and religions are the expansion of neighborhoods.

Is warring tribalism what we want our young people to learn? Or can family simply be loved ones extending their love and inclusion to the rest of society?

Love Starts Where Your Feet Are

Peace and war start within one's own home. If we really want peace for the world, let us start by loving one another within our families. Sometimes it is hard for us to smile at one another.

Mother Teresa,
No Greater Love, On Love

Honor Thy Father and Mother

If they are honorable.

Ray Fisher, *Unpublished Works*

Kindness Is Learned—or Not— at Home

When the individual families have learned kindness, then the whole nation has learned kindness. When the individual families have learned courtesy, then the whole nation has learned courtesy…Therefore, the ordering of the national life depends on the regulation of one's home life.

Confucius, *Ethics and Politics, VII*

PARENTS
AND FAMILY

Passion

Passion

Passion is intensity, energy, not only for sex but for all of living. How can you love anything or anyone without passion? The dictionary's meanings of the word 'passion' include 'to suffer', as well as 'devotion', 'intense driving feeling', 'desire', 'affection', 'anger', and 'enthusiasm'.

Passion Is Not Just Sex

For most of us, passion is employed only with regard to one thing, sex; or you suffer passionately and try to resolve that suffering. But I am using the word passion in the sense of a state of mind, a state of being, a state of your inward core, if there is such a thing, that feels very strongly, that is highly sensitive—sensitive alike to dirt, to squalor, to poverty, and to enormous riches and corruption, to the beauty of a tree, of a bird, to the flow of water, and to a pond that has the evening sky reflected upon it. To feel all this intensely, strongly, is necessary. Because without passion life becomes empty, shallow, and without much meaning. If you cannot see the beauty of a tree and love that tree, if you cannot care for it intensely, you are not living.

J. Krishnamurti,
What Are You Doing with Your Life?
Books on Living for Teens, Ch. 6

PASSION

Loving Passion Is Right Action

Intense emotion compelling action.

Webster's New Collegiate Dictionary, 1977

Compassion Is to Care Passionately

Sympathetic consciousness of others' distress together with a desire to alleviate it.

Webster's New Collegiate Dictionary, 1977

Not to Care Passionately Is a Crime

I think it pisses God off if you walk by the color purple in a field somewhere and don't notice it.

Alice Walker (1944-),
African American novelist
The Color Purple

To Care Is to Be Passionate about Life, Dignity, Equality

That man...says that women need to be helped into carriages, and lifted over ditches, and to have the best place everywhere. Nobody ever helps me into carriages, or over mud puddles, or gives me the best place, and aren't I a woman?...I have plowed and planted, and gathered into barns, and no man could head me—and aren't I a woman? I could work as much and eat as much as a man (when I could get it), and bear the lash as well—and aren't I a woman? I have born thirteen children and seen them most all sold off into slavery, and when I cried out with a mother's grief, none but Jesus heard—and aren't I a woman?

That...man...says women can't have as much rights as man, cause Christ wasn't a woman. Where did your Christ come from?...From God and a woman. Man had nothing to do with him.

Sojourner Truth [Isabella Van Wagener] (1797-1883), African American activist/philosopher *Speech, Women's Rights Convention, 1851*

PASSION

131

Passion

Passion and Compassion Are a Better High than Drugs against Depression, Loneliness, and Despair

I also think that the greater the force of your altruistic attitude towards sentient beings, the more courageous you become. The greater your courage, the less you feel prone to discouragement and loss of hope. Therefore, compassion is also a source of inner strength.

The Dalai Lama, *The Dalai Lama's Book of Wisdom*

Without Passion, You Are a Dead Person

A wrongdoer is often [someone] who has left something undone, not always one who has done something.

Marcus Aurelius (121-180),
Roman philosopher
Meditations, IX, 5

Pleasure: Fun, Excitement, Escape

Sex, drinking, drugs, music, movies, theater, church and temple entertainments, sports, shopping, clothes, cars, gambling, overeating, books—all pleasures help us escape from ourselves and our sufferings—but dependence follows.

Entertainment Is Nice: but Is It Enough?

You are quite satisfied with pleasures. There is no place for happiness. Empty your cup and clean it. It cannot be filled otherwise. Others can give you pleasure, but never happiness...

There is no East and West in sorrow and fear. The problem is universal—suffering and the ending of suffering. The cause of suffering is dependence and independence is the remedy.

Nisargadatta Maharaj,
I Am That, Ch. 91

Pleasure, Fun, and Entertainment Are Not Wrong: Only Our Misuse and Abuse of Them to Try to End Our Psychological Pain

Q: I find all this seeking and brooding most unnatural.

M: Yours is the naturalness of a born cripple. You may be unaware but it does not make you normal. What it means to be natural or normal you do not know, nor do you know that you do not know.

Q: Why is there so much suffering in the world?

M: Selfishness is the cause of suffering. There is no other cause.

Nisargadatta Maharaj,
I Am That, Ch. 91

PLEASURE: FUN, EXCITEMENT

Pleasure Depends on External Factors: People; Places; Possessions—Happiness Is an Attitude, Not a Feeling, or a Passing Sensation—You Can Feel Temporarily Awful, and Still Be a Happy Person

...I really hope no white person ever has cause
to write about me
because they never understand
Black love is Black wealth and they'll probably talk about my hard childhood
and never understand that
all the while I was quite happy.

> Nikki Giovanni (1943-),
> African American poet,
> *Nikki-Rosa*

Happiness Is a Byproduct of Right Living, Not of Pleasure

Morality is not properly the doctrine of how we may make ourselves happy, but how we may make ourselves worthy of happiness.

> Immanuel Kant (1724-1804),
> German philosopher
> *Critique of Practical Reason*

Unforeseen Side Effects

Whereas evolution depends on history, Mother Nature is no snob... Mother Nature (the process of natural selection) is famously myopic and lacking in goals. Since she doesn't foresee at all, she has no way of worrying about unforeseen side effects.

> Daniel C. Dennett,
> *Consciousness Explained*

Our pleasures are dictated by our genetic heritage: they were once based on survival (we ate what was nutritious, not poisonous, we had sex to obey the need of our genes to reproduce, our own brains provided endorphins to combat pain)—but any pleasures not based on survival may kill us.

Popularity: Power: Status

Every time people seek power over others, use popularity, wealth, fame, good looks, intellectual gifts, status (whether parent, teacher, president, football hero, or homecoming queen) to dominate or impress others, it is bullying. Actually, power only exists if you believe in it. Power, prestige, popularity—if you don't want to be exploited by these, don't be dependent on others for security or approval.

Why Use Power and Talent to Promote the 'Me'?

The selfish mind is very cunning. Either it is brutally and openly selfish or it takes many forms. If you are a politician the selfishness seeks power, status, and popularity...If you are a tyrant it express itself in brutal domination...If you are... religious it takes the form of... dogma. It also expresses itself in the family...Fame, prosperity, good looks form a basis for this creeping movement of the self...

J. Krishnamurti,
Letters to the Schools, Vol. 1

We Can Do Good Work without Self-Importance

It is the same with the scientists, with the philosophers and the professors in the university. The doer of good works, the saints and gurus...have transferred the egotism to their labors.

J. Krishnamurti,
Letters to the Schools, Vol. 1

We Confuse Status with Function

The moment you speak from status you are actually destroying the human relation.

J. Krishnamurti,
Letters to the Schools, Vol. 1

Power Is Dangerous

As long as there are sovereign nations possessing great power, war is inevitable.

Albert Einstein, on the Atomic Bomb, *Atlantic Monthly, 1945*

Approval-Seeking

The Master seemed quite impervious to what people thought of him. When the disciples asked how he had attained this stage of inner freedom, he laughed aloud and said, "Till I was twenty I did not care what people thought of me. After twenty I worried endlessly about what my neighbors thought. Then one day after fifty I suddenly saw that they hardly ever thought of me at all. "

Anthony de Mello, *One Minute Wisdom, Autonomy*

Socrates, the Fountain of Western Wisdom, Was Put to Death for Unpopularity— Afterwards They Built a Statue of Him

Socrates was judged [and condemned to death] by five hundred men of limited intelligence who harbored irrational suspicions...
It would be as naive to hold that unpopularity is synonymous with truth as to believe that it is synonymous with error.

Alain de Botton,
The Consolations of Philosophy, Ch. 1

The Puffery of It All

Sits he on never so high a throne, a man still sits on his bottom.

Michel Montaigne (1533-1592),
French essayist
Essays, Book III, Of Experience

Misuse of Power and Ordinary Rules Aren't the Same Thing

Don't argue with traffic cops, break school laws, refuse to do the dishes. It's a waste of time to go to jail, get grounded, be rude for the wrong reasons. Rules for the common good and power-mongering are not the same thing.

Ray Fisher, *Unpublished Works*

Fear Makes Us All Power and Control Addicts: Powerlessness Is, Profoundly, a Fact—We Have No Ultimate Control Over People, Places, Things— Let Go and You Are Free!

Admission of powerlessness is the first step in liberation.

Bill Wilson, *Twelve Steps and Twelve Traditions, Step One*

POPULARITY: POWER: STATUS

137

Purpose of Life

Life is a shock, rocketing between joy and pain. We are taught skills to make a living, but not skills in living or the purpose of living. These are questions human beings have asked forever:

1. *Why are we here?*

2. *Who's in charge?*

3. *Why life hurts, angers, bores us so much of the time?*

4. *What are we supposed to do about it?*

5. *If nothing, if only to bear it, is there a point to all this pain?*

6. *If the universe (God, Allah, Brahmin, Great Spirit, Buddha, Tao) is benign, how come there are babies being maimed?*

7. *If the universe is malign, why don't we all just kill ourselves now and have done with it?*

8. *Is it possible to change ourselves to feel and cause less pain?*

9. *Can one human being make a difference?*

And...

1. *Are we alone in this universe, on this rock rattling through space?*

2. *Why is my brain trying to drive me insane with its crazy thoughts?*

3. *Is my very self the mind-altering chemical that sets off so much bizarre neuronal circuitry?*

We Seek Meaning Only When We Are Confused, Unhappy: In Life's Perfect Moments, We Are Happy Just to Be Alive and Living Itself Is the Meaning of Life

Surely a man who is living richly, a man who sees things as they are and is content with what he has, is not confused; he is clear, therefore he does not ask what is the purpose of life. For him the very living is the beginning and the end. Our difficulty is that, since our life is empty, we want to find a purpose and strive for it...Therefore our purpose is how to make our life rich, not with money and all the rest of it but inwardly rich.

J. Krishnamurti,
What Are You Doing with Your Life?,
Books on Living for Teens Ch. 7

The Purpose of Life Is Loving All Life

Life is love and love is life.

Nisargadatta Maharaj,
I Am That, Ch. 22

Living, not 'Me', Is the Meaning of Life

As long as you take yourself to be a person, a body and a mind, separate from the stream of life, having a will of its own, pursuing its own aims, you are living merely on the surface and whatever you do will be short-lived and of little value, mere straw to feed the flames of vanity...Look at the content of your mind. You are what you think about. Are you not most of the time busy with your own little person and its daily needs?

Nisargadatta Maharaj,
I Am That, Ch. 95

We Are Not Separate from the Purposes of Life

It is not that we have life in us, it is life that has us in it.

Ray Fisher, *Unpublished Works*

PURPOSE
OF LIFE

Purpose of Life

The Purposes of Life Are Clearly to Live—and to Live with Compassion—Care for Others Keeps Us Alive—Be Cruel to Others, They'll Kill Us—In the Long Run, Compassion Is More Practical

For whoever would save his life will lose it, and whoever loses his life...will find it. For what will it profit a man, if he gains the whole world and forfeits his life?

Jesus of Nazareth,
Bible, Matthew 16: 25-26

Life (God, Yahweh, Allah, Brahmin, the Great Spirit, Tao) Brings the Miseries to Self-Centered People Who Are Afraid of Losing What They Have or Not Getting What They Want

I will punish the world for its evil,
and the wicked for their iniquity;
I will put an end to the pride of the arrogant,
and lay low the haughtiness of the ruthless.
I will make men more rare than fine gold...

Isaiah of Judah (c. 740-701 B.C.),
Hebrew prophet
Bible, Old Testament, Isaiah 11-12

PURPOSE OF LIFE

The Purpose of Life Seems to Be Understanding that How Much We Suffer Depends on Us

The nature of man is usually quiet, but when it is affected by the external world, it begins to have desires... When man is constantly exposed to the things of the material world which affect him and does not control his likes and dislikes, then he becomes overwhelmed by the material reality and becomes dehumanized or materialistic...and man is submerged in his own desires. From this arise rebellion, disobedience, cunning and deceit, and general immorality. We have then a picture of the strong bullying the weak, the majority persecuting the minority, the clever ones deceiving the simpleminded, the physically strong going for violence, and the sick and crippled not being taken care of, and the aged and the young and helpless not cared for. This is the way of chaos...[not of life.]

Confucius, *Discourses on Social Order*

Life Is Our Action in Relationship to Self, Others, Work, Animals, Nature: If We Love, There Is Purpose—If We Do Not Love, There Is None

Can you, mating with heaven,
Serve as the female part?

Lao Tzu, *The Way of Life*, 10

He who is useful is infinite.

Lao Tzu, *The Way of Life*, 16

PURPOSE
OF LIFE

❝ Men at some time are masters of their fates: The fault, dear Brutus, lies not in our stars But in ourselves. **❞**

William Shakespeare, *Julius Caesar*

Questioning —————————————

Questioning

Questioning

Curiosity is among our most human of adaptations. We gather information like squirrels gather nuts. We want to know everything. "Why, mommy?" is our first question after we are born, and our last question when we die. In between, we keep on asking, "What is this for? How does it work? Where did it come from? What are its uses? Will it hurt me?" The human brain craves understanding. We want to understand not only the world around us, but our own nature.

I Want to Know

"I want to know how God created this world. I am not interested in this or that phenomenon, the spectrum of this or that element. I want to know His thoughts. The rest are details," said Albert Einstein, who laid the groundwork for the twentieth century's two fundamental theories: general relativity and quantum theory.

Yet the great physicist, like his successor, theoretical physicist Stephen Hawking, sought not only science's holy grail the Theory of Everything, but what Hawking calls 'the mind of God.'

Scientists, like the rest of us, want to know how this world got created, and if there is something called God behind this creation. The interesting question is, how do we find out? Through the scientific spirit? Through the religious spirit? Or are these, in fact, the same?

Kishore Khairnar,
In and Out of Your Mind:
Teen Science: Human Bites,
Dale Carlson

QUESTIONING

Biological Evolution and Cultural Evolution Have Designed Our Brains

The mind is a system of organs of computation, designed by natural selection to solve the kinds of problems our ancestors faced in their foraging way of life, in particular, understanding and outmaneuvering objects, animals, plants, and other people...the brain processes information, and thinking is a kind of computation.

...The mind is an adaptation designed by natural selection, but that does not mean that everything we think, feel, and do is biologically adaptive.

...Biological evolution...has been superseded by cultural evolution.

Steven Pinker,
How the Mind Works, Ch. 1

Evolutionary Psychology, Biology, Genetics, Neuroscience, Sociology, Religion, Even Astrology— We Search Everywhere for Reasons for Our Bad Behavior or Our Bad Luck

Men at some time are masters of their
 fates:
The fault, dear Brutus, lies not in our
 stars,
But in ourselves.

William Shakespeare,
Julius Caesar, I:ii

Understanding Our Behavior

In this scientific age, "to understand" means to try to explain behavior as a complex interaction among (1) the genes, (2) the anatomy of the brain, (3) its biochemical state, (4) the person's family upbringing, (5) the way society has treated him or her, and (6) the stimuli that impinge upon the person.

Steven Pinker,
How the Mind Works, Ch. 1

Many of Our Questions About Ourselves Are Difficult to Answer Because the Brain Cannot See Its Own Functioning—We Can Only See Ourselves in Observing and Questioning the Way We Think, Feel, Behave in Relationship to Others, Work, Money, Things, Events

We have three principal means: observation of nature, reflection, and experiment. Observation gathers the facts, reflection combines them, experiment verifies the result of the combination.

Denis Diderot (1802-1877),
French philosopher
On the Interpretation of Nature

QUESTIONING

Any cause of behavior, not just the genes, raises the question of free will and responsibility. The difference between explaining behavior and excusing it is an ancient theme of moral reasoning, captured in the saw "To understand is not to forgive. "

147

The Science of Deduction

When you have eliminated the impossible, whatever remains, however improbable, must be the truth.

Sherlock Holmes (Sir Arthur Conan Doyle, 1859-1930, English writer), *The Sign of the Four*

To Quote Socrates Again—We Must Question Our Lives

The unexamined life is not worth living.

Socrates, *Dialogues*

As Felix Unger Said

To ass/u/me anything without questioning makes an ass out of you and me.

Neil Simon (1927-), American playwright *The Odd Couple*

The Ultimate Question

My goal is simple. It is a complete understanding of the universe, why it is as it is and why it exists at all.

Stephen Hawking, *Washington Post, 1988*

Your Philosophy Here...

"Everyone to whom much is given, of them much will be required."

Jesus of Nazareth, *Luke 12:48*

Relationships

Religion: Religious Life: Spirituality

Relationships

It is not necessary to be lonely: There are more than six billion of us, most of us huddled together in bunches. Yet strangely, we live and feel isolated. Why? What goes wrong with relationships? Do we make too many demands? Are we really entitled to vampirize, colonize, use another human being? Do we have self-isolating images of ourselves? Why do we treat a loving relationship as if we expected a return on an investment, instead of a state of communion, affection, with no ulterior motives, no goals? Why don't we understand that love simply loves!

Possessive Dependency Is Not Love

Life cannot be without relationship, but we have made it so agonizing and hideous by basing it on personal and possessive love. Can one love and yet not possess? You will find the true answer not in escape, ideals, beliefs but through the understanding of the causes of dependence and possessiveness. If one can deeply understand this problem of relationship between oneself and another, then perhaps we shall understand and solve the problems of our relationship with society, for society is but the extension of ourselves.

J. Krishnamurti,
What Are You Doing with Your Life?
Books on Living for Teens,
Section 4, Ch. 1

Why Are We Hurt in Relationship?

Why are you hurt? Self-importance, is it not? And why is there self-importance?

Because one has an idea, a symbol of oneself, an image of oneself, what one should be, what one is or what one should not be. Why does one create an image about oneself?...What awakens anger is that our ideal, the idea we have of ourselves is attacked...But when you are observing the actual fact of what you are, no one can hurt you.

J. Krishnamurti,
What Are You Doing with Your Life?
Books on Living for Teens, 4, 1

RELATIONSHIPS

153

Relationships

Why Do We Run Away Just Because There Is Pain in Relationship?

Relationship is inevitably painful, which is shown in our everyday existence. If in relationship there is no tension, it ceases to be relationship and merely becomes a comfortable sleep-state, an opiate—which most people want and prefer...if you seek security in relationship, it becomes an investment in comfort, in illusion—and the greatness of relationship is its very insecurity...

... Relationship is a process of self-revelation, of self-knowledge. This self-revelation is painful, demanding constant adjustment, pliability of thought-emotion. It is a painful struggle, with periods of enlightened peace...

J. Krishnamurti,
The Book of Life, March 1

Look at Your Relationship to Work, Sports, Playing Music, Writing Poems, Animals, Nature, Schoolwork, Friends, Family, the World Around You—Do You Love at All? Or Just Want to Get Something? True Relationship to Anything Is Love

My friends, how desperately do we need to be loved and to love. When Christ said that man does not live by bread alone, he spoke of a hunger. This hunger was not of the body...for bread [but] a hunger that begins deep down in the very depths of our being.

Love is something you and I must have. We must have it because our spirit feeds upon it...Without it our courage fails. Without love we can no longer look out confidently at the world. We turn inward and begin to feed upon our own personalities, and little by little we destroy ourselves...

With it, and with it alone, we are able to sacrifice for others.

Chief Dan George (20th c.),
Coast Salish
Wisdom of Native Americans, editor,
Kent Nerburn, Ch. 6

Religion: Religious Life: Spirituality

Are these the same? Is it necessary to go to mass, do puja, perform rituals, pray five times a day, honor ancestors' graves to live a religious life, to have an awakened spirit? What is a religious life?

Being Religious Is in How You Live

Our sisters and brothers work for the poorest of the poor—the sick, the dying, the lepers, the abandoned children...The poor are great people; they can accept very difficult things. The indifference of the people who walk by without picking up those whom we pick up is a confirmation of their ignorance and lack of faith. If they were convinced that the one who is lying on the ground is their brother or their sister, I think they would undoubtedly do something. Unfortunately, they do not know what compassion is...

Try to put worship into practice in your life...The Church is each one of us—you and I.

Mother Teresa,
No Greater Love, Ch. 11

Churches, Temples, Mosques, Pipe Ceremonies, All Reverent Rituals, Prayers, Chants, Meditation Practices, and Ceremonies Can Quiet the Brain. But, Connecting the Spirit to the Universe, God, Allah, Brahmin, Buddha Is Up to You

When you go apart to be alone for prayer, put from your mind everything you have been doing or plan to do. Reject all thoughts, be they good or be they evil. Do not pray with words unless you are really drawn to this...See that nothing remains in your conscious mind save a naked intent stretching toward God.

St. John of the Cross (1542-1591),
Spanish saint / theologian
The Ascent of Mount Carmel

RELIGION:
RELIGIOUS LIFE

There Are No Paths to Truth, God, the Universal Spirit: This Comes When Thought Is Quiet: But People Can Take Many Paths into that Quiet

The Indian saints Kabir and Tulsi Dass, as well as St. Teresa, showed an incredibly intense yearning and love for God. Ramana Maharshi... showed the path...through the method of self-inquiry...Tibetan sages Padmasambhava and Milarepa embodied...tremendous powers in the service of humanity. Jesus reflected the purest love, compassion, and sacrifice. Buddha showed the path of insight. All these are different routes to a single goal... liberation.

"In any way that men love me in that same way they find my love: for many are the paths of men, but they all in the end come to me." —Bhagavad Gita 4: 11

Ram Dass,
Journey of Awakening, Ch. 4

What All Great Religious Teachers Make Clear, Is that Religious Ritual and Religious Living Are Not the Same: A Spiritual Inner Life Means Behaving with Kindness, Not Just Going to a Particular Building or Reading a Particular Book

A certain Bektashi dervish was respected for his piety and appearance of virtue. Whenever anyone asked him how he had become so holy, he always answered: "I know what is in the Koran."

One day he had just given this reply to an inquirer in a coffee-house, when an imbecile asked: "Well, what is in the Koran?"

"In the Koran," said the Bektashi, "there are two pressed flowers and a letter from my friend Abdullah."

Ram Dass,
Journey of Awakening,
Idries Shah, *Ch. 7*

Religion: Connection and Behavior

Li [religion] is the principle of mutual respect and courtesy. Therefore when it is applied to worship at the temples, we have piety...when applied to the home, we have affection between parents and children and harmony between brothers; when applied to the village, we have respect for order...

Confucius, *The Wisdom of Confucius, First Discourse*

Prayer and Ritual Are Not Enough

You shall be rewarded according only to your deeds.

Mohammed, *Koran, The Ranks,* 37: 42

Religion: It's What You Do

I call saintliness not a state but the moral procedure leading to it.

Jean Genet (1910-1986), French philosopher Quoted by Jean Paul Sartre *in Saint Genet, 1952*

RELIGION: RELIGIOUS LIFE

❝ Men flourish only for a moment. **❞**

Homer, *Odyssey*

Self

Self

Sex

Success

Suffering

Self

What is the self? Thought invents what we call our SELF, to give us a sense of security, of definition, so we have the feeling we're not falling apart all the time. We have lots of selves, actually. All those voices in our heads that keep arguing with each other, are all the different selves from all the different stages of our lives…Then the collective SELF, while it thinks it is keeping you safe, becomes an armed prison from which it is hard to escape, and through whose windows we peer out.

The Self Is Actually Only a Story We Tell Ourselves— There's Nobody Home in Any of Us: We Are Made of Atoms and Universal Life—Seeing This Is Freedom from the Loneliness of Separation, of Living in the Black Box of Mental Prison

The need for self-knowledge extends beyond the problems of identifying the external signs of our own bodily movement. We need to know about our internal states…we build up a defining story about ourselves…And what is this thing [the self]? It's nothing more than, and nothing less than, your center of narrative gravity… you are the program that runs on your brain's computer…

Daniel Dennett, *Consciousness Explained*, Ch. 13

The Self Is What We Think and Feel in the Moment, Not Some Separate or Continuous Mini-Me—Watch the Movement of Your Self: There Are Gaps When 'You' Are Not There

For my part, when I enter most intimately into what I call myself, I always stumble on some particular perception or other, of heat or cold, …love or hatred, pain or pleasure. I can never catch myself at any time without a perception, and can never observe anything but the perception…[Someone else] may, perhaps, perceive something simple and continued, which he calls himself; though I am certain there is no such principle in me.

David Hume (1711-1776), Scottish philosopher *Treatise on Human Nature, 1739*

SELF

Self

Our Warring Inner Selves Produce Outer Wars: Listen to the Voices Arguing in Your Head: They Produce the Anger and Fear In Us We Take Out on Everybody Else—Through Attention, Self Can End for Moments at a Time

The sense of continuity and solidity of self is just an illusion. There is really no such thing as ego, soul or atman. It is a succession of confusions that create ego. The process which is ego actually consists of a flicker of confusion, a flicker of aggression, a flicker of grasping—all of which exists only in the moment. Since we cannot hold on to the present moment, we cannot hold on to me and mine and make them solid things...The experience of oneself...is actually a fleeting thought. If we generate these fleeting thoughts fast enough, we can create the illusion of continuity and solidity.

Chogyam Trungpa,
The Myth of Freedom, Ch. 1

The Self Is Just the Sum of Our Memories—We Are the Nerds with Brains that Invent Self-Importance as a Survival Tool, as Other Creatures Have Fur or Claws

The brain and the [elephant's] trunk are products of the same evolutionary force...We are chauvinistic about our brains, thinking them to be the goal of evolution. And that makes no sense, for reasons articulated...by Stephen Jay Gould [who says we are only a twig somewhere on the bush of life, not the top of its tree]...natural selection does nothing even close to striving for intelligence.

Steven Pinker,
How the Mind Works, Ch. 3

Sensitivity Is Not the Same as Self-Protective Touchiness: It Is An Outward Movement of Being Aware of Others, of Nature, of the Universe

Receptive to sense impressions... Delicately aware of the attitudes and feelings of others.

Webster's New Collegiate Dictionary

SELF

162

Sex

Why do we make such a big issue of sex, whether it is heterosexual or homosexual? Sex is as natural as eating or sleeping. It's a healthy, accessible, affordable pleasure. It is an instant escape from our troubles. It isn't sex that's the problem—it is our thinking about sex that creates the problem.

What's the Big Deal?

What do we mean by the problem of sex? Is it the act, or is it a thought about the act? Surely, it is not the act. The sexual act is no more a problem to you any more than eating is a problem to you, but if you think about eating or anything else all day long because you have nothing else to think about, it becomes a problem to you...Why do you build it up, which you are obviously doing? The cinemas, the magazines, the stories, the way women dress: everything is building up your thoughts of sex. And why does the mind build it up; why does the mind think about sex at all?...

Why has it become a central issue in your life? When there are so many things calling, demanding your attention, you give complete attention to the thought of sex. What happens; why are your minds so occupied with it? Because that is the way of ultimate escape, is it not? It is a way of complete self-forgetfulness.

J. Krishnamurti,
What Are You Doing with Your Life?
Books on Living for Teens, IV, 2

St. Paul Also Says It Is the Obsession, the Burning that Is the Problem, Not Sex

It is better to marry than to burn.

Paul of Tarsus,
Bible, 1 Corinthians 7: 9

SEX

Sex and Work, Says Freud, Give Us the Greatest Pleasure, Best Ward Off Suffering and the Pitiless Threat of Death

The feeling of happiness derived from the satisfaction of a wild instinctual impulse...is incomparably more intense than that derived from satisfying an instinct that has been tamed...

Another technique for fending off suffering is the employment of...displacements [shifting the energy] of libido [sex drive]...

Sublimation [diverting the sex drive to something more culturally acceptable] of the instincts...can...heighten the yield of pleasure from the sources of psychical and intellectual work...such as an artist's joy...or a scientist's in solving problems or discovering truths.

Sigmund Freud,
*Civilizations and Its
Discontents, Ch. 1*

Sex Is the Genes' Way of Reproducing Themselves

People don't selfishly spread their genes; genes selfishly spread themselves. They do it by the way they build our brains...by making us enjoy life, health, sex, friends, and children...Sexual desire is not people's strategy to propagate themselves. It's people's strategy to attain the pleasures of sex, and the pleasures of sex are the genes' strategy to propagate themselves. If the genes don't get propagated [by abstention or by contraception], it's because we are smarter than they are.

Steven Pinker,
How the Mind Works, Ch. 7

Why Is There Sex to Begin with? Sexual Reproduction (the Union of Two Parents) Is a Healthy Advance on Asexual Duplication

A man and a woman need each other's DNA and hence can enjoy sex. A man and a woman have a common interest in their children and their enduring love has evolved to protect that interest. And a husband and wife can be each other's best friends, and can enjoy the lifelong dependability and trust that underlies the logic of friendship. These emotions are rooted in the fact that if a man and woman are monogamous, together for life…their genetic interests are identical.

Steven Pinker,
How the Mind Works, Ch. 7

Homosexuality: Nature or Nurture?

The argument against persecuting gay people must be made not in terms of the gay gene or the gay brain but in terms of people's right to engage in private consensual acts without discrimination or harassment.

Steven Pinker,
How the Mind Works, Ch. 1

Heterosexuality: Nature or Nurture?

Men and women. Women and men. It will never work.

Erica Jong (1942-),
American writer
Fear of Flying

SEX

Success

[See also: Failure]

Might as well enjoy what we do: moments of actual success don't last.

Now Is Always: Everything Else Passes

Men flourish only for a moment.

> Homer (c. 700 B.C.),
> Greek epic poet
> *Odyssey, Bk. XIX, 328*

The Moment of Success Is Often Followed by a Small Death

Achievement, n. the death of endeavor and the birth of disgust.

> Ambrose Bierce (1842-1914),
> American writer
> *The Devil's Dictionary*

Everyone Has Her or His Moment

In the future everyone will be world-famous for fifteen minutes.

> Andy Warhol (1927-1987),
> American artist
> *Photo Exhibition Catalog*

What Is Success?

Other people can talk about how to expand the destiny of mankind. I just want to talk about how to fix a motorcycle. I think that what I have to say has more lasting value.

> Robert Maynard Persig, American writer/philosopher
> *Zen and the Art of Motorcycle Maintenance. III, 25*

166

People Who Want Success Are Always Afraid They May Not Be Good Enough

The ambitious man is the most frightened man because he is afraid to be what he is, because he says, "If I am what I am, I shall be nobody. Therefore, I must be somebody, I must become the engineer, the engine driver, the magistrate, the judge, the minister. "

J. Krishnamurti,
What Are You Doing with Your Life?
Books on Living for Teens, II, 7

Ambition Is Wanting the World's Reward for Success— Interest Is Loving the Work for Itself

Now, if I am interested…in being an engineer because I love it, because I want to build beautiful houses, because I want to have the best irrigation in the world, because I want to build the best roads, it means I love the thing; therefore, that is not ambition. In that, there is no fear.

J. Krishnamurti,
What Are You Doing with Your Life?
Books on Living for Teens, II, 7

SUCCESS

Suffering

Life can be beautiful—so why do we hurt?

Life does hurt. Even though we do what we think we're supposed to do, we still don't feel good inside.

Life is a glorious joy, too, of course, what with sunsets, music, falling in love. But it still comes as a shock, especially in the teen years when so much is good and exciting, how much life can confuse and just plain hurt sometimes.

It hurts from fear, loneliness, from anger, despair, from being poor, or emotionally ill. It hurts from violence, whether in the street from crime, or at home or at school, from failing, depression, self-hate, rejection, envy, feeling different, being bullied.

The trouble is most of us never get taught to expect pain. We don't know where the pain is, where it comes from, and what to do about it. We never get taught that it isn't so much life, but our brains' reactions to life that cause the pain.

We're taught to want things, to hate and fear—and then our brains come up with solutions that cause even more pain, drugs, alcohol, sex, violence. If your brain isn't going to kill you, you will have to pay attention to what it is doing, and how it is reacting to everything. That's the important meditation—to pay attention.

Pain and hurt are part of life. Poverty, war, physical pain will happen. Somebody will die. We will fail, be rejected, feel lonely, left out, even in a crowd of friends. We will fear death or sickness, feel pity for our own life or the poor and sick of the world. It is thought's fear of pain and its effects on the very self thought has invented, that turns into long-term suffering.

Nobody tells us pain passes. But you can use your awareness of the brain's processes to get over emotional pain.

Everyone Suffers for a While from Loss or Pain—But Ongoing Psychological Suffering Is a Self-Centered Activity—The Measure of Love Is Not Suffering but Giving

True love is love that causes us pain, that hurts, and yet brings us joy...God...wants us to give ourselves to each other until it hurts.

Mother Teresa,
No Greater Love, Ch. 2

Psychological Suffering Is Truly Optional: Try to Let Go of, or at Least Not Hang on to, Some Psychological Hurt: Experiment with This for Yourself

Someone has not loved you, hurt your feelings, rejected you. Think of this as getting a sharp elbow in the ribs. The bruise will hurt a while. Then it will pass—if you let it. Just change the channel when thoughts of the hurt come into your head. You can choose your thoughts as you choose your friends—let go of the bad ones, keep the good ones.

Ray Fisher,
Unpublished Works

SUFFERING

 **Suffering**

Some People Think We Learn from Suffering, Deserve Suffering, and Come to Love the Self-Pity of Suffering if Not the Pain Itself

Cause there's somethin' in a Sunday
That makes the body feel alone.

Kris Kristofferson,
Sunday Mornin' Comin' Down

Is There Something Delicious about Psychological Suffering?

Man is sometimes extraordinarily, passionately, in love with suffering.

Fyodor Dostoyevski,
Notes from the Underground

What Do We Learn from Pain Except How to Stand Pain?

No pain, no gain.

Anonymous

Some People Think We Learn Joy Better from Joy

It is not true that suffering ennobles the character; happiness does that sometimes, but suffering, for the most part, makes men petty and vindictive.

W. Somerset Maugham
(1874-1965), English Writer
The Moon and Sixpence

Do Not Suffer Fools Gladly

Living life as art requires a readiness to forgive. I do not mean that you should suffer fools gladly, but rather remember your own shortcomings.

Maya Angelou,
Wouldn't Give Nothing
for My Journey Now

Pain and Suffering

Pain happens; suffering is optional.

Old Saying, Anonymous

Don't Suffer Silently

Do not go gentle into that good night,
Old age should burn and rage at close
of day;
Rage, rage against the dying of the
light.

Dylan Thomas (1914-1953),
British poet,
Do Not Go Gentle
into that Good Night

SUFFERING

❝ An eye for an eye, and soon the whole world will be blind. ❞

Mahatma Gandhi, *Speech*

Teaching

Teaching

Thoughts and Thinker

Truth

Teaching

The most important job on the universe's job approval list is teaching. In nature, our very lives depend on the instructions of our own DNA molecules, then on our parents to teach us how to begin staying alive, then on teachers to civilize our immature, instinct-driven behaviors long enough to learn skills to go on staying alive.

But teaching is a two-way dialogue, a two-way responsibility. If we are not learning, is there such a thing as teaching? And except for facts, techniques, skills in trades and professions, can anyone teach another skills in living, or insight into the problems of life?

We Must Be Careful What We Teach

A teacher affects eternity; he or she can never tell where his or her influence stops.

Henry Adams (1838-1918),
American writer
The Education of Henry Adams, Ch. 20

The Art of Teaching

The whole art of teaching is only the art of awakening the natural curiosity of young minds.

Anatole France (1824-1924),
French writer
The Crime of Sylvestre Bonnard

Life Teaching

Some say you should do nothing without the help of a teacher... Others say that a teacher is not necessary, that you can only do it yourself. Of course, people have awakened and come to full realization without any teacher. On the other hand, most people at some point along the path need teachers.

Ram Dass,
Journey of Awakening, Ch. IV

TEACHING

175

Catch Fire from the Teaching: Carry the Torch—Don't Build an Altar to the Fire

Be lamps unto yourselves. Be a refuge unto yourselves. Do not turn to any external refuge. Hold fast to the teaching as a lamp.

Buddha,
The Pali Canon

Teaching Is Not Yelling at Other People

There is always so much to be distressed about in human behavior that you can remain in eternal conflict battling with this and that. And at the end of eighty years or so you discover that your main accomplishment was to have remained in conflict for so long. The conflict can be within or without; it doesn't really matter. It's still war.

Ray Fisher,
Unpublished Dialogues

Is Anyone Listening to Teachers Anyway?

Probably, no. Most good materials remain unread, unstudied, unexamined. It is for the person who lives, speaks, writes, to ask the questions or make the significant statements for themselves. Whether or not others take them seriously is irrelevant. There has been so much incredibly good insight. Ultimately, it was for the speakers themselves... that changes happened, or there were further insights. Krishnamurti spoke for sixty-five years, the Buddha spoke for x years, Christ for x years... then think of all the books that have been published since time began. Who is listening, who is reading?

R. E. Mark Lee, *Letter*

TEACHING

Thoughts and Thinker

The trouble with thought is, it thinks that's all there is in the brain. Thought, as we have discovered, is simply the response of memory, lots of memories, knowledge, the past, what was learned a long time ago, what was learned five minutes ago.

We have also seen that thought invents what we call our SELF, to give us a sense of security, of definition, so we have the feeling we're present. And, because the job of the brain is to protect the organism, to keep it alive, it makes and remembers images...helps us remember not to hang around lions.

Thought has its place, of course.

But also, as we have seen, the brain does two things not just one. It thinks—and it understands. Thought (old stuff) and intelligence (right-now understanding, observation) are separate functions. Thought, often called intellect, makes science, for instance—intelligence tells you what is the right or wrong thing to do with it.

It's Important to Understand the Limits of Thought

A human being is part of the whole that we call the universe, a part limited in time and space. He [or she] experiences himself, his thoughts and feelings, as something separate from the rest—a kind of optical illusion of his consciousness. This illusion is a prison for us, restricting us to our personal desires and to affection for only the few people nearest to us. Our task must be to free ourselves from this prison.

Albert Einstein, *Speech*

Our Thoughts about People and Things Prevent Us from Seeing Their Reality Clearly— Just as We Make Up a Self, We Make Up People and the World as We Go Along

Awareness is a vantage point from which you can focus on any event...Take, for example, your relationship with your parents [boyfriend, girlfriend]...Your parent [boyfriend, girlfriend] comes along and says something to which you immediately react and [they] in turn react to you. These are habitual reactions...in which nobody really listens; there is merely a mechanical run-off between people. If you are rooted quietly in your awareness [not your thoughts], there is space, ...you see the reaction you would usually make. But you also see the situation in a variety of other ways...You might see that your parent [boyfriend, girlfriend] is in fact...like you.

Ram Dass,
Journey of Awakening, Ch. 1

Thinking and Feeling Are Necessary: It Is the Presence of the 'Thinker/Feeler' and Its Past Thoughts and 'Felts' that Stand Between Us and What Is Going on

Much of our inner dialogue...is this constant reaction to experience by a selfish, childish protagonist. None of us has moved very far from the seven-year-old who vigilantly watches to see who got more.

"Pay precise attention, moment by moment, to exactly what you are experiencing, right now, separating out your reactions from the raw...events." This is what is meant by bare attention...allowing things to speak for themselves as if seen for the first time.

Mark Epstein,
Thoughts without a Thinker, Ch. 6

Just Look without Thoughts Chattering and You'll See Yourself

There is no emotional experience, no mental event, no disavowed or estranged aspect of ourselves that cannot be worked with through the strategy of bare attention...coming to terms with the unwanted, unexplored, and disturbing aspects of our being.

Mark Epstein,
Thoughts without a Thinker, Ch. 6

Thought Invents the Self

Perceiving the impermanency of thoughts, thought itself creates the thinker who gives himself permanency. So thought creates the thinker and not the other way about...There is only thought, and the bundle of thoughts creates the 'me', the thinker.

J. Krishnamurti,
What Are You Doing with Your Life? Books on Living for Teens

THOUGHTS
AND THINKER

Truth

Scientists now say they can use technology to prove the truth philosophers have been pointing out: that even if it feels like there is a self inside our heads, the self has no location in the brain or any other part of the body. So, since the truth isn't to be found inside your head, where is truth to be found?

Scientists and metascientists both seem to suggest truth is found in silence, in attention to our connection to the universe and just the joy, the pain, the experience in being alive. We seem to discover that truth and god, the sky and the birds that fly in it, and we ourselves are one.

Are You in There?

The trouble with brains, it seems, is that when you look in them, you discover that there's nobody home. No part of the brain is the thinker that does the thinking or the feeler that does the feeling.

Daniel C. Dennett,
Consciousness Explained, Ch. 2

Searching for Freedom Doesn't Work

The truth shall make you free.

John, *Bible, New Testament, 8: 32*

Loving Attention, not Organized Thought

Truth is a pathless land. Man cannot come to it through any organization, through any creed, through any dogma, priest or ritual, not through any philosophic knowledge or psychological technique. He has to find it through the mirror of relationship, through the understanding of the contents of his own mind, through observation and not through intellectual analysis...His perception of life is shaped by the concepts already established in his mind...This content is common to all humanity...

When there is negation of all those things that thought has brought about psychologically, only then is there love, which is compassion and intelligence.

J. Krishnamurti,
from Krishnamurti: The Years of Fulfillment: the Core of the Teachings,
Vol. 2 of his biography
by Mary Lutyens

Most People Are Looking for Comfort and Permanency, not Truth

Truth is not the result of an effort, the end of a road. It is here and now...you do not see it because you look too far away from yourself...Truth is not a reward for good behavior, nor a prize for passing some tests...You are eligible because you are. You need not merit truth. It is your own. Just stop running away by running after. Stand still, be quiet.... Truth is in the discovery, not in the discovered. And to discovery there is no beginning and no end.

Nisargadatta,
I Am That, Ch. 74

TRUTH

“We must have the courage to fight back. But we must use the weapon of love. Even if people hurt you, you must hurt no one. No lie can live forever. ”

Martin Luther King, Jr., *Speech*

Violence

Violence

Violence

Human violence and nature's struggle among plants and animals for survival are not the same. The lion rests when he has mates and enough food and territory to survive. Humans seem to want more than enough of everything, especially power. It's as if we want more security than is possible. In our fear, we have become the most brutal, the most dangerous species on the Earth—even to each other. We fear and hurt even other humans who are weak, different, in the minority.

But to change all this, we need, not more violence, but active nonviolence.

We Beat Up on Each Other Even in Countries Where There Is Political Freedom

The second brute fact about the American past and present is that this society is a chronically racist, sexist, homophobic and jingoistic one. The complex and tortuous quest for American identity from 1776 to our own time has produced a culture in which people define themselves physically, socially, sexually and politically in terms of race, gender, sexual orientation and 'anti-American' activities...

American liberalism...leaves... untouched...forms of social misery: the maldistribution of resources, wealth and power...the extension of American liberalism in regard to race, labor, women, gays, lesbians and nature.

Cornel West (1953-),
African American
intellectual/philosopher
The Cornel West Reader, Ch. 16

VIOLENCE

Violence

We Must Use Active Nonviolence to Change Laws, not Just More Mayhem

An eye for an eye, and soon the whole world will be blind.
If they kill me, they will have my body—not my obedience.
I am willing to die—but not to kill.
Resistance must never be passive.
Resistance must be active—I want to change their minds, not kill them.
Poverty is the worst form of violence.

[Mahatma: Great Soul] Mohandas Gandhi (1869-1948), Indian political philosopher: from *Speeches in the Fight to Free India from White British Rule*

The Antidote to Violence Is Right Education

But the chief problem in any community cursed with crime is not the punishment of the criminals, but the preventing of the young from being trained to crime...I have seen twelve-year-old boys working in chains on the public streets...directly in front of the schools, in company with old and hardened criminals; and this indiscriminate mingling of men and women and children makes the chain-gangs perfect schools of crime and debauchery.

It is in the public schools, however, which can be made, outside the homes, the greatest means of training decent self-respecting citizens.

W. E. B. du Bois,
The Souls of Black Folks, Ch. 9

Martin Luther King, Jr. Taught Active Nonviolence to Free African Americans from White American Rule—as Gandhi Did India from White British Rule—He Believed, as Gandhi Believed, that White Leaders Would Tire of All the Trouble and Change the Laws

Act with calm and loving dignity. But
    do not obey unfair laws.
We must have the courage to fight
    back. But we must use the
    weapon of love.
Even if people hurt you, you must
    hurt no one.
No lie can live forever.

Martin Luther King, Jr.
Speeches and Sayings

What Do We Do When We Are Hurt?

No one teaches us what to do when we are hurt. So we do what humans have always done: either take it out by destroying someone else, or take it out by destroying ourselves. There is a third way. We have mouths, we can talk. We are the animal with language. Buddha, Jesus, and Mother Teresa had tempers. They did not go around smacking people. They talked and talked, and talked, and talked. Even Helen Keller didn't hit people over the head with her cane when they acted as if her brains were in her eyeballs. She fought for people with disabilities with words.

Edgar M. Bick, M. D., *Letters*

VIOLENCE

Violence

Language Is a Better Tool than Violence

The mystery of language was revealed to me. I knew then that 'w-a-t-e-r' meant the wonderful cool something that was flowing over my hand. That living word awakened my soul, gave it light, joy, set it free!

Helen Keller (1880-1968),
American activist
The Story of My Life

Jesus Threw the Furniture Around When He Was Angry, or Turned the Other Cheek, which Made His Antagonists Crazy, So They Paid Attention

You have heard that it was said, 'An eye for an eye and a tooth for a tooth.' But I say to you, Do not resist one who is evil. But if any one strikes you on the right cheek, turn to him the other also.

Jesus of Nazareth,
Bible, New Testament,
Matthew 5: 38-39

War, Terrorism, Crime—Why Are We Such a Danger to Ourselves?—Why Don't We Get It that If We Hurt Other People, We Get Hurt? Society's Violence Begins in Each One of Us and Spreads: Change Yourself—It's as Catching as Colds

But a new world is necessary. A new culture is necessary. The old culture is dead, buried, burnt, exploded, vaporized. You have to create a new culture. A new culture cannot be based on violence. The new culture depends on you because the older generation has built a society based on violence, based on aggressiveness and it is this that has caused all the confusion, all the misery. The older generations have produced this world and you have to change it. You cannot sit back and say, "I will follow the rest of the people and seek success and position." If you do, your children are going to suffer.

J. Krishnamurti,
On Education, I, 7

Really!

There never was a good war or a bad peace.

Benjamin Franklin (1706-1790),
American statesman/
scientist/philosopher,
Letter to Josiah Quincy

What Does War Decide Anyway?

War doesn't decide who is right. It decides who is left.

Unknown, contributed by
Jessica Baycroft, age 17,
American student

VIOLENCE

189

❝That man says women can't have as much rights as man, cause Christ wasn't a woman. Where did your Christ come from?…from God and a woman. Man had nothing to do with him.**❞**

Sojourner Truth, *Women's Rights Convention Speech*

Wisdom ————————————————————————

Wisdom

Work

Wisdom

The word 'wisdom' may be a false word. It suggests a body of knowledge, and knowledge is a past collection of information which may or may not be true. To be wise means, it seems, always to be attentive and clear in the moment about what it is appropriate to do. To be wise is, therefore, not cumulative.

We Can Be Wrong for Eighty Years

The older I grow the more I distrust the familiar doctrine that age brings wisdom.

H. L. Mencken (1880-1956),
American wit and philosopher
Prejudices, Third Series

To Be Wise Is to Have Universal Attitudes

My country is the world and my religion is to do good.

Thomas Paine (1737-1809),
American philosopher
The Rights of Man, Ch. 5

Wisdom

To Preach One Thing, Think Another, and Do a Third, Is Not Wise

Whilst you are proclaiming peace and good will to men, emancipating all nations, you insist upon retaining an absolute power over wives…and notwithstanding all your wise laws and maxims we have it in our power…to free ourselves.

Abigail Adams (1744-1818),
American First Lady
Letter to John Adams

A Wise Mind Is an Open One

Minds are like parachutes. They only function when they are open.

Sir James Dewar (1842-1923),
Scottish experimental scientist
Attributed

Wisdom May not Be a Matter of 'Wise' Words

What wisdom can you find that is greater than kindness?

Jean Jacques Rousseau (1712-1778),
French philosopher
Emile; or, On Education, I

WISDOM

Work

We have a right to work in the pursuit of life, liberty, and in the pursuit of happiness, but only in ways that do not hurt the equal rights and safety of other people in pursuit of the same things. Humans are a social, herd, pack animal—our need to work, to contribute, to be valuable is a matter of survival, not only for our daily bread, but so we will be valued by and not left out of the pack to die.

We have supermarkets now. We don't have to be competitive killers to drink at the waterhole with the other animals. So why do we go on competing for everything?

Everyone Has the Right to Work

We hold these truths to be self-evident; that all men [and women] are created equal; that they are endowed by their creator with certain inalienable rights; that among these are life, liberty, and the pursuit of happiness.

Thomas Jefferson (1743-1826),
American president/writer
Declaration of Independence,
July 4, 1776

Few People Know More about Work than the Missionaries of Charity

I'm just a little pencil in God's hand.

Mother Teresa,
No Greater Love, Ch. 4

WORK

Work

Work is a Gift

To the world, it seems foolish that we delight in poor food...possess only three sets of habits made of coarse cloth...enjoy walking in any shape and color of shoes; bathe with just a bucket of water...go hungry and thirsty but refuse to eat in the houses of other people...walk distances in the rain and hot summer sun, or go cycling, travel...third-class over-crowded trains; sleep on hard beds...kneel on the rough and thin carpets in the chapel...work like coolies at home and outside when we could easily employ servants and do only the light jobs...To some we are wasting our precious life and burying our talents...

Our beautiful work with and for the poor is a privilege and a gift to us...

God loves me. I'm not here just to fill a place, just to be a number. He has chosen me for a purpose. I know it.

Mother Teresa,
No Greater Love, Ch. 11

All Work, Everyone's Work, Is Equally Important, although Growing Tomatoes May Be Slightly More Useful than Writing a Book

I am the people—the mob—the crowd—the mass.
Do you know that all the great work of the world is done through me?

Carl Sandburg, (1878-1967),
American poet
Poems 1916

We Once Worked Only to Find Food, Clothing, Shelter: Now It Measures Our Worth

The great law of culture is: Let each become all that he [or she] was created capable of being.

Thomas Carlyle (1795-1881),
Scottish essayist/historian
Critical and Miscellaneous Essays

WORK

Why Do We Use Comparison of Status, Wealth, Ability to Turn Young People into Competitive Killers for a Place in the Sun—Instead of Helping Teenagers to Find Work They Love and to Love Their Work

Work is love made visible. And if you cannot work with love but only with distaste, it is better that you should leave your work and sit at the gate of the temple and take alms of those who work with joy.

Kahlil Gibran (1883-1931),
Syrian poet
The Prophet: on Work

Everything We Do Counts

All work, even cotton spinning, is noble; work is alone noble...

Thomas Carlyle,
Past and Present

Work Not Paid for, or Paid for Unequally for Reasons of Gender, Color, Sexual Preference, Religion, Is Slavery

The facts are that women [and minorities] do not get equal pay for equal work, though economic and social trends have forced women to become breadwinners all over the world...Those breadwinners still work the 'second shift' at home. And now they face a future, including their old age, with no guarantees for their security.

Pamela McCorduck and Nancy Ramsey (20th c.),
American authors
The Futures of Women: Scenarios for the 21st Century, Introduction

Money Is Necessary to Live: But It Is the Work that Counts

Labor is prior to, and independent of, capital. Capital is only the fruit of labor, and could never have existed if labor had not first existed. Labor is the superior of capital, and deserves much the higher consideration.

> Abraham Lincoln (1809-1865),
> American president/political
> philosopher
> *First Annual Message to Congress*

The Integrity of Work—Life Is Not a Popularity Contest

I desire so to conduct the affairs of this administration that if at the end, when I come to lay down the reins of power, I have lost every other friend on earth, I shall at least have one friend left, and that friend shall be down inside me.

> Abraham Lincoln,
> *Reply to the Missouri Committee*

The Unlucky Must Work Where They Can, but Even They Can Discover What They Like to Do

To find out what you love to do demands a great deal of intelligence; because, if you are afraid of not being able to earn a livelihood, or of not fitting into this rotten society, then you will never find out. But, if you are not frightened, if you refuse to be pushed into the groove of tradition by your parents, by your teachers, by the superficial demands of society, then there is a possibility of discovering what it is you really love to do. So, to discover, there must be no fear of not surviving.

> J. Krishnamurti,
> *What Are You Doing with Your Life?*
> *Books on Living for Teens, III, 3*

In the End

In the end, philosophy means a search for understanding, of values and what is real. It is a love of the truth for its own sake, not for gain or approval, not for safety or security, but because the truth matters. As we see, the religious spirit, the philosophy spirit, and the science spirit are all based on the same things: observation, experimentation, and learning for oneself.

What is important, what is everlasting, what is timeless? This will only mean something to you if you find out for yourself.

WORK

"When elephants fight, it is the grass that suffers. **"**

Kikuyu Proverb

Selected Biographies and Philosophies

Selected Biographies and Philosophies

Some of these philosophers are from out of history, some recent, some are living right now. Some are religious philosophers, some political philosophers, some science philosophers. Some are women, some men, of all cultures, colors, countries, who understood that the truth was the only thing worth having.

Buddha, the root meaning of which is to be awake, intelligent, wise, was the name given to the Indian prince Gotama (563-483. B.C.), when, after leaving the palace and renouncing riches, earthly kingdom, family, and after years of spiritual struggle, he awoke to the understanding of the source of human suffering, and freedom from it—nirvana. He found escape from psychological pain through understanding that suffering arises from self-centered living, that right living is the way out. But instead of remaining in his bliss, he returned to teach all humanity.

Confucius, from K'ung Futse, meaning 'Master Kung' (551-479 B.C.) was the great Chinese teacher, who, like Socrates, wrote no books himself (Plato and others recorded the words of Socrates), but whose teachings affected not only Chinese but world ethical history. Confucius said, very much like Buddha, that the happiness of the world, the country, the family is based on the right behavior of each one of us. 'Confucian classics' consist of *The Five Classics* and *The Four Books*. Confucius also contributed the *Commentary to King Wen's Book of Changes (I Ching).*

Einstein, Albert was a theoretical physicist (1879-1955). His Theory of Relativity, Special Theory of Relativity, his search for a Unified Field Theory all represent the scientist's search for an explanation of the universe in a single mathematical formula. For Einstein, as for Stephen Hawking, current leading theoretical physicist (1942-), the search for the

SELECTED BIOGRAPHIES

physical origin of and explanation for the universe is essentially the metaphysical search for the mind and the mystery of god.

Sigmund Freud (1856-1939) was a neurologist and founder, in the Western world, of the philosophical psychology that the self, both conscious and unconscious, is the origin of our suffering and our problems.

Jesus of Nazareth—Jewish religious philosopher born between 8 B.C. and 4 B.C. near the end of Herod's reign, and crucified about 29 B.C.because everybody was angry with him for rebelling against religious, political, and conventional hypocrisy. God and religion were serious matters to him. Heaven, like Buddha's nirvana, was a matter of living in the absence of self and in the presence of God: the meek (not the power-hungry egotist) shall inherit. As world teacher/religious philosopher, he spoke and disciples recorded. Disciples founded the Christian religion based on his message (see New Testament: Four Gospels), especially the Sermon on the Mount. Jesus is Greek for Joshua, his Hebrew name: the word Christ is the Greek word for messiah, the ideal human who teaches humanity about the best in us.

Immanuel Kant (1724-1804) was a German metaphysicist who described the limits of human knowledge. Kant knew there are two capacities in the human brain, insight that is infinite—and knowledge, which is limited to our brain's *a priori*—we have a 4-dimensional view of the universe only: height, depth, width, and what Einstein later called space-time. In other words, we do not see reality objectively, but only through our imaging system, our 'I' experience of three real and one imaginary dimension. This is a major breakthrough in our understanding of the limits with which the human brain perceives the world, the universe—and each other!

Martin Luther King, Jr. (1929-1963) was the political visionary philosopher whose life was sacrificed for civil rights. He understood how profoundly equal all human beings are, regardless of color, country, class, that we are all connected, and if any of us suffer, we all suffer. To this end, his great understanding that change must occur without violence—with active, not passive protest like marches and boycotts, but without violence, echoed the teachings of Jesus long ago, and Mahatma Gandhi in this century. He voiced his teachings perfectly in his 1963 speech *I Have a Dream*, and in 1964 won the Nobel Peace Prize.

Krishna, Lord Krishna, appears to the hero Arjuna in the Hindu Vedanta, the Bahagavad-Gita, written 2, 500 years ago, to reveal what we now call the Perennial Philosophy, the Hindu exposition of a way of life that appears again and again throughout civilization, in Plato's Dialogues, in the Bible, in Confucius, Buddha, today in the teachings of Krishnamurti. Human beings who understand and control their desires, who live for all and not just for themselves, may perhaps have physical pain but will not suffer psychologically.

Krishnamurti, Jiddu (1895-1986) is the twentieth century's world religious teacher/philosopher. He wrote several books himself, and until the age of ninety, he traveled the world speaking to large audiences, leading scientists, professors, students. His talks and dialogues are published in more than fifty books in many languages. Krishnamurti's legacy is profoundly significant to our modern world: we must rise above the traditions and beliefs, the separative sense of self and the personal that are the basis for our fear, greed, violence—and find out what it means to be truly free. Self-knowledge, understanding the ways of the self historically, biologically, personally—this is the key to being free of the suffering they cause, not listening to any authority, especially the authority of the past. Understanding is attention in every moment to our reactions and behavior in relationship, and is the beginning of wisdom, of the eternal.

Lao Tzu, born in China in 604 B.C., left us about eighty brief verses called *The Way of Life, The Tao*—possibly the

SELECTED
BIOGRAPHIES

sweetest, simplest, loveliest version of the Perennial Philosophy in human legacy. Like the Sermon on the Mount or Krishnamurti's Talks, the *Way of Life* is easy to read and hard to live. Like Jesus, Lao Tzu was a rebel: he spurned authority, and said humans must live, not according to ritual, but in accord with the conscience of the universe.

Mohammed, born in Mecca (570-632 A.D.), was the Arabian prophet who was appalled at the low condition of his people, struggled against ancient Arabic tribal customs, raised his people through teaching them the principles now embodied in the *Koran*, and founded Islam as a world religion with Mecca as its center. Islam has in common with the teachings of Moses and Confucius, an emphasis on the authority of law and custom, rather than individual insight.

Moses, Jewish political leader, lawgiver, and philosopher of about 1200 B.C., who led the Israelites out of Egypt and across the Middle East

deserts to Canaan. He founded a country and a philosophical/religious/political/cultural nation for the Jews, leaving his teachings and laws—including The Ten Commandments—in the *Five Books of Moses*, the first five books of the *Bible*'s Old Testament. Like Confucius, Moses was primarily concerned with the ritual tradition of correct conduct, with rational law, with obedience to the authority of religious law, family custom, cultural usage rather than individual interpretation and insight into the conscience of the universe.

Plato (427?-347 B.C.), disciple of Socrates and teacher of Aristotle, the Greek philosopher who founded the Academy, a school of philosophy based on Socratic dialogue. His works include *Republic*, *Laws*, *Timaeus*, subjects ranging from justice to the theory of the universe.

Chief Seattle (1786-1866) of the Squamish and Duamish Tribe, gave a speech in 1853 more quoted and revered than any other by a Native American political philosopher. He tried to teach the white man (unsuccessfully) that all humans are the same family, that all things are connected, and that "whatever befalls the earth befalls the children of the earth."

Socrates (470?-399 B.C.) was a Greek philosopher, a rebel, like Jesus after him, who was publicly killed (forced to drink a cup of poison) for his teachings. His greatest contribution to Western civilized inquiry was the dialogue: a way of coming to the truth through a series of questionings, not just the acceptance of second-hand information called authority. We still call this kind of question/answer the Socratic method.

Mother Teresa (1910-1997), religious philosopher, was born Agnes Gonxha Bohaxhiu, in Yugoslavia, and later sent to India as a Catholic nun. She became, even before she won the Nobel Peace Prize, one of the world's most recognized and beloved spiritual leaders. Like Krishnamurti, Jesus, and Buddha,

she was a rebel. She founded the order of the Missionaries of Charity because she felt and taught that compassion for the destitute dying as well as for the rich, the blind and disabled as well as the whole, the outcast as well as the wellborn, was the whole point in living. Her philosophy was that God is inside us all, that joy is based on service to others. It was simple: be a pencil in the hand of God. And give till it hurts.

Sojourner Truth (1797-1883), an electrifying African American political philosopher who escaped slavery, helped others to escape, became an activist for African American women's rights in what was then only sought for white middle-class women. She took on the problem of black female invisibility, and, in 1851 at the women's rights conference, gave her famous "Aren't I a Woman?" speech—three years before her association with Abraham Lincoln.

<blockquote>
" As I see it today, the ability to read awoke inside me some long dormant craving to be mentally alive. "

Malcolm X, *The Autobiography of Malcolm X* as told to Alex Haley
</blockquote>

Bibliography and Suggested Reading ————

BIBLIOGRAPHY

Bibliography and Suggested Reading

Many of the philosophers and their works, whose insights are helpful in understanding and comparing our human history of trying to puzzle out our lives and the world we live in, are mentioned in the text. The works listed here are very accessible to anyone, even those with no religious, political, science, or philosophy background. While most are not written for young adults, as this book Who Said What? definitely has been, they are very readable, easy to poke around in and read bits of. They are often humorous, and very helpful in just living through the problems of everyday life.

Primary Sources

Buddha. *The Dhammapada* (Teachings). Translated by Juan Mascaro. London, England: Penguin Books, 1973. "In the Dhammapada we can hear the voice of Buddha," says Mascaro. The brief 65 pages of Buddha's message on the way to live life, good and evil, pleasure, freedom, are simply translated, with a clear explanatory introduction, and comparisons to Confucius and Lao Tzu.

Confucius. Editor and translator, Lin Yutang. *The Wisdom of Confucius.* New York: Random House, Modern Library, 1943. The life and philosophy of Confucius is well and simply presented: The Golden Mean, ethics, politics, harmony in living, education of the young.

Jesus of Nazareth. *Bible*: New Testament. Any version.

Krishna, Lord. *The Song of God: Bhagavad-Gita.* Translated by Swami Prabhavananda and Christopher Isherwood, Introduction by Aldous Huxley. New York: Penguin Books, New American Library, 1972. The philosophic, religious epic is the most popular in Hindu religious literature, as it encapsulates the way of life much as Moses did in the Ten Commandments, Plato did in the Dialogues, Jesus did in the Sermon on the Mount, Lao Tzu did in The Tao, Buddha in The Teachings. God is everything, everything is God; humans are capable of knowing God, not through reason but insight; the purpose of life is connection with God and the universe. All this, Lord Krishna tells the hero Arjuna in this section of *The Mahabarata*, the equal of our Old Testament as the *Gita* is rather like our New Testament. This edition makes the Gita accessible.

J. Krishnamurti. *What Are You Doing with Your Life?—Books on Living for Teens*. Ojai, California: Krishnamurti Publications of America, 2001. Teens learn for themselves about the great world teacher's philosophy: about relationships, about education and work, about the whole purpose of life. Through paying attention to their conditioning in their daily lives, not through listening to any psychological authority (which does not mean freedom to do anything you like) with insight teens can find out the meaning of love, money, ambition, violence, and by changing violence in themselves, they can change the world.

Lao Tzu. *The Way of Life*. Translated by Witter Bynner. New York: Penguin-Putnam Inc., 1986. Confucius called Lao Tzu a dragon, a creature he would never understand, an individual, not a conformist. This is the way of poise, assurance, how to work with the forces of nature, our own psyches, other people, to live a more successful life as an individual.

Mohammed, *The Koran*. (*Qu'ran*, meaning The Recital). Translated by N. J. Dawood. New York: Penguin Putnam Inc., 1999. The earliest and finest work of classical Arabic prose, for Muslims the Word of God revealed to the Prophet Mohammed by the Angel Gabriel. Its most important tenet is submission to the will of God as revealed in the laws of the *Koran* to Islamic religious leaders.

Moses. *Bible*, Old Testament, especially the first Five Books. Any version.

Mother Teresa, *No Greater Love*, Foreword by Thomas Moore. Edited by Becky Benenate and Joseph Durepos. Novato, California, New World Library, 1997. The essential wisdom of Mother Teresa, on love, prayer, giving, service. Sections on the Missionaries of Charity; a biographical sketch, and a conversation with Mother about her work with the poor and the dying.

General Sources for Quotations

Bartlett, John. *Familiar Quotations.* 16th edition. Boston, New York, London: Little, Brown and Company, 1992. A most famous source of quotations, drawn from religions, literature, history, science, philosophy. John Bartlett became famous as an information bank for quotations.

Carlson, Dale. *Stop the Pain: Teen Meditations.* Madison, CT: Bick Publishing House, 1999. Self-knowledge is true meditation: ways to lose the anxiety, hurt, conflict, pain, depression, addiction, loneliness, and to move on. See also *Where's Your Head? Psychology for Teenagers.* 2nd edition. Madison, CT: Bick Publishing House, 1998. A general introduction for young adults to the structure of personality formation, the meaning of intelligence, the mind, feelings, behaviors, biological and cultural agenda, and how to transform our conditioning and ourselves.

Dass, Ram (Richard Alpert). *Journey of Awakening: A Meditator's Guidebook.* Revised edition. New York: Bantam Books, 1990. This American psychologist and philosopher is also a spiritual teacher who discusses in this book the many religious/philosophical teachings aimed at finding and understanding the truth.

Haber, Louis. *Black Pioneers of Science and Invention.* New York, London: Harcourt Brace Jovanovich, Publishers, 1970. These African American philosopher/scientists performed the first open-heart surgery, proved that blood from a black soldier would not turn a white man black (all humanity has the same blood types), and played crucial roles in the world's science and attitudes.

Kaplan, Rob, editor. *Science Says: A Collection of Quotations on the History, Meaning, and Practice of Science.* New York: W. H. Freeman and Company, 2001. Today, we look to interpreters of science as well as religious philosophers for wisdom, for insights into the nature of the universe, who we are, and common explanations for the world in which we live. Quotes range from Aristotle to Einstein, Kant to Hawking, Freud to Armstrong on the moon. Not a single great black scientist is mentioned. For African American pioneers in science and their thoughts, see Louis Haber's *Black Pioneers of Science and Invention,* above.

All things are connected. Whatever befalls the earth, befalls the children of the earth.

Chief Seattle, *Speech*

Index

Index

INDEX

BICK PUBLISHING HOUSE
PRESENTS
Books for Teenagers
Science & Philosophy

Who Said What?
Philosophy Quotes for Teens
by Dale Carlson. Pictures by Carol Nicklaus

Teen guide to comparing philosophies of the great thinkers of the ages: form your own philosophy.

"Thought-provoking guide." —School Library Journal

NEW! Illustrations, Index, 256 pages, $14.95. ISBN: 1-884158-28-5

In and Out of Your Mind
Teen Science: Human Bites
By Dale Carlson. Edited by Kishore Khairnar, M.S. Physics

Teens learn about our minds, our bodies, our Earth, the Universe, the new science—in order to make their own decisions. This book makes science fun and attainable.

"Heady stuff." — School Library Journal

NEW! Illustrations, Index, 256 Pages, $14.95. ISBN: 1-884158-27-7

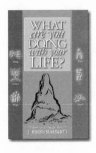

What Are You Doing with Your Life?
Books on Living for Teenagers
By J. Krishnamurti. Edited by Dale Carlson

Teens learn to understand the self, the purpose of life, work, education, relationships.

The Dalai Lama calls Krishnamurti "one of the greatest thinkers of the age." *Time* magazine named Krishnamurti, along with Mother Teresa, "one of the five saints of the 20th century."

Illustrations, Index, 288 Pages, $14.95. ISBN: 1-888004-24-X

BICK PUBLISHING HOUSE
PRESENTS
Books for Teenagers
Psychology & Meditation
by Dale Carlson • Hannah Carlson, M.Ed., CRC
NEW EDITIONS

Stop the Pain: Teen Meditations
New York Public Library Books 2000 List
Independent Publishers Award
Teens have their own ability for physical and mental meditation to end psychological pain.

- What Is meditation: many ways
- When, where, with whom to meditate
- National directory of resources, centers

"Much good advice...." — *School Library Journal*

Illustrated, indexed, 224 pages, $14.95; ISBN: 1-884158-23-4

Where's Your Head?
Psychology For Teenagers
New York Public Library Books 2000 List
YA Christopher Award Book

- Behaviors, feelings, personality formation
- Parents, peers, drugs, sex, violence, discrimination, addictions, depression
- Joys of relationship, friends, skills
- Insight, meditation, therapy

"A practical focus on psychological survival skills."
— *Publishers Weekly*

Illustrated, indexed. 320 pages, $14.95; ISBN: 1-884158-19-6

Girls Are Equal Too
The Teenage Girl's How-to-Survive Book
ALA Notable Book
The female in our society: how to change.

- Girls growing up, in school, with boys
- Sex and relationships
- What to do about men, work, marriage, our culture: the fight for survival.

"Clearly documented approach to cultural sexism."
— *School Library Journal*

Illustrated, indexed, 256 pages, $14.95; ISBN: 1-884158-18-8

BICK PUBLISHING HOUSE
PRESENTS
Books for Health & Recovery

The Courage to Lead
Start Your Own Support Group:
Mental Illnesses & Addictions
By Hannah Carlson, M.Ed., C.R.C.

Diagnoses, Treatments, Causes of Mental Disorders, Screening tests, Life Stories, Bibliography, National and Local Resources.

"Invaluable supplement to therapy."
— *Midwest Book Review*

Illustrated, indexed, 192 pages, $14.95; ISBN: 1-884158-25-0

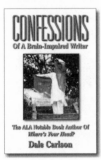

Confessions of a Brain-Impaired Writer
A Memoir By Dale Carlson

"Dale Carlson captures with ferocity the dilemmas experienced by people who have right hemisphere learning disabilities...she exposes the most intimate details of her life....Her gift with words demonstrates how people with social disabilities compensate for struggles with relationships."

— Dr. Kathleen C. Laundy, Psy.D., M.S.W.,
    Yale School of Medicine

224 pages, $14.95, ISBN: 1-884158-24-2

Stop the Pain: Adult Meditations
By Dale Carlson

Discover Meditation: You Are Your Own Best Teacher
How to use meditation to end psychological suffering, depression, anger, past and present hurts, anxiety, loneliness, the daily problems with sex and marriage, relationships, work and money.

"Carlson has drawn together the diverse elements of the mind, the psyche, and the spirit of science...Carlson demystifies meditation using the mirrors of insight and science to reflect what is illusive and beyond words."

—R.E. Mark Lee, Director, Krishnamurti Publications America

Illustrations, 288 pages, $14.95; ISBN: 1-884158-21-8

BICK PUBLISHING HOUSE
PRESENTS

Books on Wildlife Rehabilitation

by Dale Carlson and Irene Ruth
Step-by-Step Guides • Illustrated
Quick Reference for Wildlife Care
For Parents, Teachers, Librarians who want
to learn and teach basic rehabilitation

**Wildlife Care For Birds And Mammals
7-Volume Compendium**
ISBN: 1-884158-16-1, $59.70

I Found A Baby Bird, What Do I Do?
ISBN: 1-884158-00-5, $9.95

I Found A Baby Duck, What Do I Do?
ISBN: 1-884158-02-1, $9.95

I Found A Baby Opossum, What Do I Do?
ISBN: 1-884158-06-4, $9.95

I Found A Baby Rabbit, What Do I Do?
ISBN: 1-884158-03-x, $9.95

I Found A Baby Raccoon, What Do I Do?
ISBN: 1-884158-05-6, $9.95

I Found A Baby Squirrel, What Do I Do?
ISBN: 1-884158-01-3, $9.95

First Aid For Wildlife
ISBN: 1-884158-14-5, $9.95

*Endorsed by Veterinarians, Wildlife Rehabilitation
Centers, and National Wildlife Magazines.*

ORDER FORM

307 NECK ROAD, MADISON, CT 06443
TEL. 203-245-0073 • FAX 203-245-5990

Name: _____

Address: _____

City: _____ State: _____ Zip: _____

Phone: _____ Fax: _____

QTY	BOOK TITLE	PRICE	TOTAL
	YOUNG ADULTS/TEENAGERS		
	Who Said What? Philosophy Quotes for Teens	14.95	
	In and Out of Your Mind: Teen Science: Human Bites	14.95	
	What Are You Doing with Your Life?	14.95	
	Stop the Pain: Teen Meditations	14.95	
	Where's Your Head?: Psychology for Teenagers	14.95	
	Girls Are Equal Too: The Teenage Girl's How-To-Survive Book	14.95	
	BOOKS FOR HEALTH & RECOVERY		
	The Courage to Lead	14.95	
	Confessions of a Brain-Impaired Writer	14.95	
	Stop the Pain: Adult Meditations	14.95	
	BOOKS ON LIVING WITH DISABILITIES		
	Living with Disabilities	59.70	
	I Have a Friend with Learning Disabilities	9.95	
	I Have a Friend with Mental Illness	9.95	
	BOOKS ON WILDLIFE REHABILITATION		
	Wildlife Care for Birds and Mammals	59.70	
	I Found a Baby Bird, What Do I Do?	9.95	
	I Found a Baby Duck, What Do I Do?	9.95	
	I Found a Baby Opossum, What Do I Do?	9.95	
	I Found a Baby Rabbit, What Do I Do?	9.95	
	I Found a Baby Raccoon, What Do I Do?	9.95	
	I Found a Baby Squirrel, What Do I Do?	9.95	
	First Aid for Wildlife	9.95	
	TOTAL		
	SHIPPING & HANDLING ($3.50)		
	AMOUNT ENCLOSED		

Send check or money order to Bick Publishing House. Include shipping and handling.

**Also Available at your local bookstore from: BookWorld,
Baker & Taylor Book Company, and Ingram Book Company**

www.bickpubhouse.com

Author

Dale Carlson

Author of over fifty books, adult and juvenile, fiction and nonfiction, Carlson has received three ALA Notable Book Awards, and the Christopher Award. She writes novels and psychology books for young adults, and general adult nonfiction. Among her titles are *The Mountain of Truth* (ALA Notable Book), *Girls Are Equal Too* (ALA Notable Book), *Where's Your Head?: Psychology for Teenagers* (Christopher Award, N.Y. Public Library Best Books List), *Stop the Pain: Teen Meditations* (N.Y. Public Library Best Books List), *Wildlife Care for Birds and Mammals*, *Stop the Pain: Adult Meditations*, and *In and Out of Your Mind: Teen Science*. Carlson has lived and taught in the Far East: India, Indonesia, China, Japan. She teaches writing here and abroad during part of each year. She makes her home among her five pre-teenage grandchildren, Chaney, Jacquelyn, Malcolm, Sam, and Shannon, and her cats in Connecticut.

Illustrator

Carol Nicklaus

Known as a character illustrator, her work has been featured in *The New York Times*, *Publishers Weekly*, *Good Housekeeping*, and *Mademoiselle*. To date she has done 150 books for Random House, Golden Press, Atheneum, Dutton, Scholastic, and more. She has won awards from ALA, the Christophers, and The American Institute of Graphic Arts.